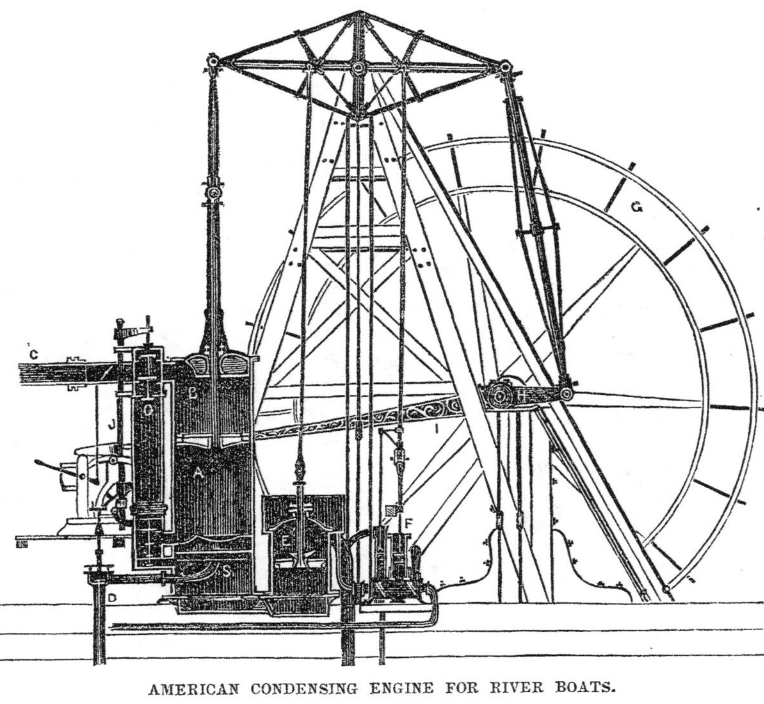

AMERICAN CONDENSING ENGINE FOR RIVER BOATS.

HISTORY

OF

PROPELLERS

AND

STEAM NAVIGATION.

WITH

BIOGRAPHICAL SKETCHES

OF THE

EARLY INVENTORS.

BY

ROBERT MACFARLANE, C. E.,

EDITOR OF THE "SCIENTIFIC AMERICAN."

NEW-YORK:

GEORGE P. PUTNAM

1851.

JOHN F. TROW, PRINTER,
49, 51 & 53 Ann-st.

DESIGN OF THE WORK.

The object of this History of Propellers and Steam Navigation is two-fold. One is the arrangement and description of many devices which have been invented to propel vessels, in order to prevent many ingenious men from wasting their time, talents, and money, on such projects. The immense amount of time, study, and money, thrown away on such contrivances, is beyond calculation. The author has had opportunities which few possessed, of viewing a vast amount of indifferent re-inventions brought out for this purpose; and it has been a subject of regret to him to know, that this was owing to the want of historical information on such subjects. This work is designed to supply, in a measure, that want. It is not pretended that it contains all the propelling devices which have been invented, but it contains the only instructive arrangement, and by far the greatest variety of such devices; and in this respect it is hoped that it will be the means of doing some good.

Another object of this work is, to present an interesting history of Steam Navigation, especially that of the attempts of the early inventors in this department of "practical mechanics." There has been much controversy respecting the claims of those men who made the first experiments in steam navigation. The author has examined the claims of each, and has treated the subject, he believes, impartially. Much information, to be found in no other work, is arranged within, relating to Fitch, Rumsey, Fulton, Symington, and Bell. A separate chapter is devoted to Marine Navigation, which will be found to contain much that is but parpartially known in our country. The different applications of the steam engine to river and sea navigation is clearly illustrated.

The author has seen a great number of experiments made with different kinds of propelling devices; his views will be obtained from the spirit pervading the book, the intention of which is to benefit those interested and engaged in such pursuits.

CONTENTS.

HISTORY

OF

PROPELLERS AND STEAM NAVIGATION.

CHAPTER I.

IN tracing the progress of every great discovery, we almost invariably find "coming events casting their shadows before." Before America was discovered, there had been handed down from generation to generation, wonderful traditions of the fabled "Atlantis." Strada described the "magnetic telegraph" nearly two centuries before it was really invented; and he also describes a floating pageant which was got up on the Tiber for the amusement of Pope Leo the Tenth, and was propelled by "six huge wheels—three on each side—which by their constant motion carried on the machine, until it arrived before the Pope's Villa." But the most remarkable olden description of a steamboat, is to be found in that exciting romance of the middle ages, "Amadis of Gaul." The unknown author, therein describes the Queen of enchanters rushing over the ocean in a fiery vessel, which bears no indistinct resemblance to the appearance of the Clermont, on her first midnight voyage, from New-York to Albany.

The most ancient vessel on record, was propelled without oars, paddle, wheels, or screw. This was the Ark of our father Noah. We must give it the precedence, in point of primogeniture, over the primitive, but ancient canoe of the Indian, who is here represented, with his paddle in hand

"Skimming Ontario's waters blue,
Like the swallow's wing, in his bark canoe."

The most ancient navigators that we have any account of, were the Phœnicians. The cities of Tyre and Carthage were famous for their fleets, and their citizens for maritime skill, such as was known in those days. To them the then distant Island of Albion was not unknown, for thither they came with their oared galleys to dig tin from ancient Cambria's hills. From all that we can correctly gather on the subject of ship propulsion, the oar was the only universal instrument used in the days of old, and a good instrument it is for that purpose, far superior, when the power applied is manual, to that of the paddle-wheel, owing to the oarsman being able to apply his power more economically than to the wheel. The application of wheels to propel boats, dates as far back as the time of the Romans, or as some say, the Egyptians, but upon this point we are not positive, therefore we have arrayed an "ancient mariner" at the wheel, as a cosmopolite, belonging to any part of the world our readers may assign

him. In 1682 Prince Rupert propelled his barge in this manner, and there are two or three other instances on record nearly as old. Of one thing we are certain, that before the introduction of steam propulsion, navigation was a slow process, and that is not long ago. If Solomon had been acquainted with such a power for propelling the ships of his fleet, they would not have taken three years to make their voyages for peacocks and *California* gold.

The great improvement which has been effected by steam power, as applied to navigation, by increasing the intercourse between people of different and distant nations, has resulted more than any other invention on record (and is still augmenting) to unite mankind, we hope, in one great family, working in concord for their common good. The steam engine may be called the grand improver of the age. Its power can be increased to almost any extent, and can be made to execute the most difficult and delicate operations. For business or pleasure, it conveys the traveller from place to place, with celerity, convenience, and economy.

The origin of the application of steam to propelling vessels is claimed by several persons of different nations. Tug vessels propelled by wheels driven by horses, were proposed and employed long before steam was thought of for that purpose. The earliest account in our possession respecting the employment of steam to propel vessels, is that of a Spanish Captain, named Blasco De Garay, who, it is said, in 1543, in the presence of Charles V., in the harbor of Barcelona, propelled a vessel of 200 tons burden, against wind and tide, at a considerable speed. The account of this vessel is taken from the Royal Archives of Simuncas, and was first given to the world in 1825. The vessel is described to have had paddle-wheels suspended on its sides, but after the experiment was made, although the emperor paid all the expenses, the inventor took out his machinery, and with the *wisdom* of all ancient inventors, left it to rot in darkness. Quite a controversy has existed among paper wasting historians, respecting the nature and construction of De Garay's steamboat, but all that we have been able to learn from an examination of many opinions about it, is nothing at all, and since De Garay has not enlightened us himself, we may justly dismiss the claims of Spain, for nothing was heard about it by the world until steam navigation had been successfully established both in America and Great Britain. The steamboat is not such a wonderful *invention* in *itself*—the steam engine, is the parent of the successful steamboat. Steamboats had been built and tried, but all were dead failures, until the improved steam engine of Watt was applied to them; with it they at once, on the Hudson, in the New World, and on the Clyde, in the Old,

"Walked the waters like things of life."

PAPIN, SAVERY, WORCESTER, ALLEN, HULLS.

DR. PAPIN, a Frenchman, Captain Savery, and the Marquis of Worcester, proposed to propel vessels by steam power applied in some way to paddles, but the testimony which is left to posterity of their contrivances for that purpose, is so unsatisfactory and vague that little can be made out of it.

In 1726, a Dr. John Allen published a work in London in which he proposed to propel a vessel by having a horizontal pipe open at the stern, into which air or water was to be forced, to propel the boat forward by its reaction. The Doctor tried his scheme on a boat upon a canal, and he states that if steam was used as a power, he had no doubt but it could be moved at the rate of three miles per hour.

The first patent on record to propel a vessel by steam power, is that of Jonathan Hulls, who published a pamphlet in 1737, describing it, and for which posterity is not a little obliged to him. Some have claimed for him very high honor. His invention is certainly a nearer approach to a steamboat than all that had been invented before him, but without an opinion expressed, for or against, his steamboat is here presented.

Fig. 3.

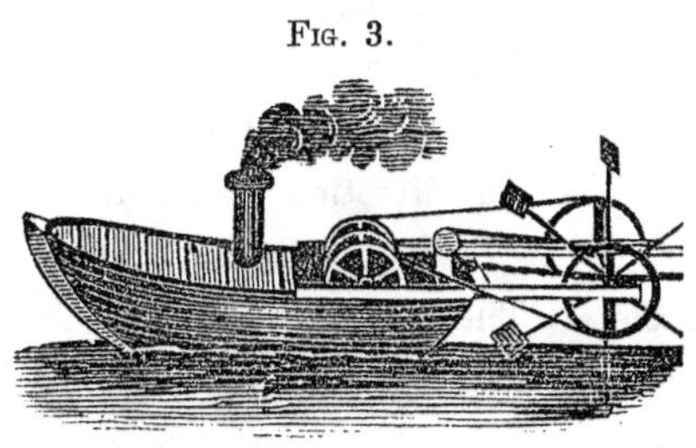

As there have been many plans brought forward as substitutes for the crank, it may be news to many, to be told that the crank was not the first contrivance used to convert a reciprocating into a rotary motion, but it was adopted from its beautiful simplicity after many other plans failed. Hulls' mode of converting the reciprocating motion of the engine into a rotary one, is depicted in the annexed diagram, fig. 4,

Fig. 4.

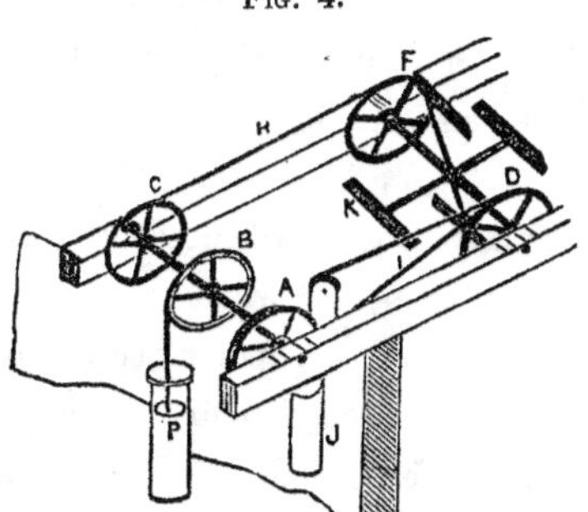

in which A, B, C, are three wheels, on one axis; and D, F, two others, hung loose on a parallel axis, with ratchet wheels attached, so as to move the axis only in the forward direction. P is the piston of an atmospheric steam engine, connected to the middle wheel, B, by a rope passing round the latter. H is another rope, connecting the wheels C, F, so that both must move in the same direction; and I is a rope which connects the wheels A, D, diagonally, so that they move in opposite directions. The rope I, proceeding from the wheel A, is continued round the wheel D, and passed over a small pulley; a weight, J, being suspended from the end of it. When the piston descends, the wheels A, B, C, move forward: and, by the ropes I, H, turn the wheels D, F; that is, the wheel F forward, and the wheel D backward. The paddles K are therefore moved round, in a forward direction, by the wheel F; while, at the same time, the weight, J, is raised by the wheel D. When the piston is, in the next place, ascending, the motion of the whole is reversed, except that of the paddles, which are moved in the same direction, by the action of the descending weight J, upon the wheel D. By this alternate action, the axis A, B, with the paddle-wheel, is constantly moved around in the same direction, and by an equable force.

This is the first paddle-wheel driven by steam power, and the idea of placing the wheel in the stern occurred to the inventor as being the proper place for it, because water fowl, ducks and geese pushed their web feet behind them.

There seems to be some discrepancy in the accounts

given of Jonathan Hulls' application of steam to propel vessels. Herbert, in his history, says that Hulls took out a patent for the application of the crank, whereas Hulls' pamphlet, from which the engravings are taken, represents another plan than the crank, to convert a reciprocating into a rotary motion, to drive the paddle-wheel. The engine of Hulls was single acting, and the application of a crank to it, has always been very difficult, as the ascending stroke has to be effected by a counterbalance, and an immense fly-wheel, not suitable to the steamboat, is necessary.

CHAPTER II.

DE JOFFRIE, RUMSEY, FITCH.

After Hulls, the steamboat slumbered, till 1782, when the Marquis De Joffrie tried one on the Loire, at Lyons in France. He used paddles, on an endless chain. It was not successful.

Fig. 5.

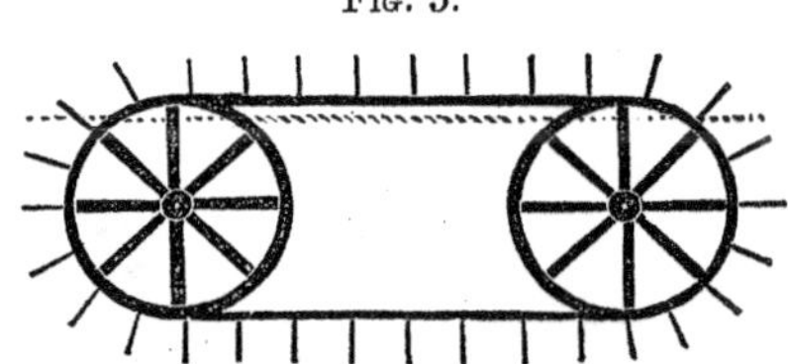

In 1784, Mr. James Rumsey, of Shepardstown, Virginia, made a private experiment with a steamboat, and in 1787 a public one, on the Potomac. Rumsey's boat was about eighty feet long, and was propelled by a steam engine which worked a vertical pump in the middle of the vessel, by which the water was drawn in at the bow, and expelled at the stern, through a horizontal trunk in her bottom. The reaction of the effluent water carried her at the rate of four miles an hour, when loaded with three tons, in addition to the weight of her engine, of about a third of a ton. The boiler held no more than five gallons of water, and needed only a pint of water at a time; and the whole machinery did not occupy a space greater than that required for four barrels of flour.

Rumsey went to England, and after two years' preparation to get a vessel afloat on the Thames, died, just as he had completed its construction. This was in 1793. The vessel made several trips on the Thames, against wind and tide, at the rate of four miles per hour. It was propelled by the reaction of water, like his first one, on the Potomac.

The contemporary of James Rumsey was John Fitch, a man of great mechanical resources and inventive powers. He published the following description of his boat, in the Columbian Magazine, December, 1786.

FIG. 6.

"The cylinder is to be horizontal, and the steam to work with equal force at both ends. The mode by which we obtain a vacuum is, we believe, entirely new, as is also the method of letting the water into it and throwing it off against the atmosphere without any friction. It is expected that the cylinder, which is twelve inches in diameter, will move with a clear force of eleven or twelve cwt., after the frictions are deducted; this force to be directed against a wheel eighteen inches in diameter. The piston is to move about three feet, and each vibration of it is to give the axis (or shaft) about forty evolutions. Each evolution of the axis moves twelve oars, or paddles, five and a half feet. They work perpendicularly, and are represented by the strokes of the paddle of a canoe; as six of the paddles are raised from the water, six more are entered, three on a side, and the two sets of paddles make their strokes of about eleven feet at each evolution. The cranks of the axis act upon the paddles about one third of their length from their lower ends, on which part of the oar the whole force of the axis is applied. The engine is placed in the bottom of the boat, about one third from the stern, and both the action and evolution turn the wheel the same way."

It is stated by Charles Whittlesley, Esq., in his pamphlet, "Justice to the Memory of John Fitch," that the first model of a steamboat, built by Fitch, had side-wheels, but the buckets of them were found to labor so hard under water, that he adopted the plan of propulsion which we have represented above; and the construction of such a boat became to him the highest object of his ambition. In the biography of John Fitch, published in the Friends' Weekly Intelligencer, by Mr. Daniel Longstreth, of Warminster,

Pennsylvania, he adheres to the point that John Fitch preferred the wheels, and adopted the paddles, which were patented by Henry Voight, once chief coiner of the United States Mint, at Philadelphia, who was one of Fitch's fundholders. Between the two accounts there is a discrepancy, but none so far as it respects the wheels being attached to his first model. We are of opinion that Fitch preferred the paddles, as they were represented in his drawings, and also a model after he secured his patent, in 1791.

James Rumsey and John Fitch were contemporaneous inventors, and no person at this day would imagine the amount of strife, ill feelings, and struggling for supremacy and for public favor there were between the two and their friends, were it not for documents left behind—(showing the value of the art of printing)—to prove the old adage with inventors as with merchants, "two of a trade cannot agree."

Fig. 7.

At the present day, when so much is said about who was the first inventor of the screw propeller, to be told it was an American—the unfortunate John Fitch—will surprise many people; but so it was. It will also surprise many to be told, that his propeller sailed in 1793, in water 60 feet deep, where the Halls of Justice now stand, in New York City. In 1846 Mr. John Hutchins, of Wesley Place, Williamsburgh, L. I., published a chart, with the above cut, which has been somewhat widely circulated in this city. Mr. Hutchins says, that in the summer of 1796 or '97, he, when a lad, assisted Mr. Fitch in steering his boat, and otherwise attending to his machinery of the boat (Fig. 7) on Collect Pond, which then covered the ground where the Tombs now stand, and that part of our city round that quarter. The boat was a common long-boat, eighteen feet in length, six feet beam. She was steered at the bow when the propeller was used. The boiler was a 10 or 12 gallon pot with a thick plank lid firmly fastened down on it. The cylinders were of wood, barrel-shaped outside, and firmly hooped. The main steam pipe was led from the boiler into a copper box. The leading pipes led into two cylinders. Each piston rod was attached to the extremity of the beam. The connecting rod is seen between the bow cylinder and the beam support. Mr. Hutchins says it was so arranged as to turn the crank of the propelling shaft, which passed horizontally through the stern of the boat and was made fast to the screw. If the above is a true cut of John Fitch's engine and its arrangement for propelling, we must conclude that the ideas for the purpose of propelling were good, but the machinery was crude, and that Mr. Fitch had not attained to the true mode of combining the mechanical for driving the propelling parts. But we must make due allowance for Fitch's poverty for the want of commanding right materials, and if he propelled the boat at the rate of six miles per hour, may we not rather be charmed with that genius which took not the materials he would have chosen, but what were at his command, and propelled his rough boat, with his rougher engine, at such an astonishing speed. We are inclined, however, to doubt the speed stated, because it is not a bad speed with a good engine and screw, at the present day. But although we have no doubts about the boat and the screw used by Fitch, as a propeller, we will be pardoned for checking one discrepancy in Mr. Hutchins' memory. He states that both Livingston, Fulton, and Col. J. Stevens visited Fitch's boat, and that Mr. Fitch explained to Fulton the *modus operandi* of the machinery. Now all the biographers of Robert Fulton assert that in 1796–7 he was in France. He went to London in 1786, and did not return to America till 1806. In 1797 he was trying experiments with Joel Barlow on the Seine, and it would be a very singular thing to find him both on the Seine, in France, and the Collect Pond, in New-York, at the same time. It would have been well had the fact of this propeller, with the date of its operation, been set forth, and no more. Herbert attributes the invention of the screw propeller to an American, but does not state the name of the inventor, and in fact nowhere before have we been able to trace this invention to its author. Mr. Hutchins has therefore done the cause of science a service in this respect. This boat, with a part of its machinery, was abandoned by

Mr. Fitch, and left to decay on the banks of the Pond, from whence it was carried away, piece by piece, by the children, for fuel.

Rumsey's plan for propelling, was entirely different from that of John Fitch, as will be perceived from the following description of his boat (Fig. 8), and it may be interesting for many to know, that since the days of Rumsey his invention has been frequently revived. It is only two years since a patent was secured at Washington by a gentleman in Baltimore (Mr. Fulton), for some principle connected with propelling by water, and since that, another to Mr. Ruthven, of Scotland. We will now describe the first invention for propelling boats by steam power, forcing a jet of water out towards the stern of the vessel.

Fig. 8.

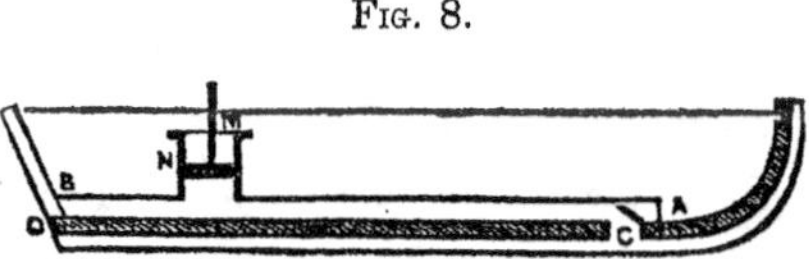

In the bottom of the boat, on the Kelson, A, there is a trunk, B, the after end of which is open, and terminates at the stern-post, D; the other end is closed, and the whole trunk, according to its dimensions, occupies about three fourth parts of the length of the boat.—On the closed end of the trunk stands a cylinder, N, two and a half feet—from this cylinder there is a communication by a tube to the river or water under the boat, by the valve, C, to admit the water from the river into the cylinder, and it likewise prevents it from returning again the same way. There is another communication which lets water pass freely from the cylinder to the trunk, through which it is discharged by the stern; on the top of this cylinder there stands another of the same length, which is fixed to the under one by screws; in each of these cylinders there is a piston, which moves up and down with very little friction; these pistons are connected together by a smooth bolt, M, passing through the bottom of the upper cylinder, acting as a pump to draw water from the river through the tube and valve, before described. The upper cylinder acts as a steam engine, and receives its steam from a boiler under its piston, which is then carried up to the top of the cylinder by the steam (at the same time, the piston of the lower cylinder is brought up to its top, from its connection with the upper piston, by the aforesaid bolt,) they then shut the communication from the boiler, and open another to discharge the steam for condensation; by this means the atmosphere acts upon the piston of the upper cylinder, and its force is conveyed to the piston in the lower cylinder, by the aforesaid connecting bolt, which forces the water, then in the lower cylinder, through the trunk, with considerable velocity; the reaction of which, on the other end of the trunk, is the power that propels the boat forward.

It is well known that a heavy body falling near the earth will pass through a space of about fifteen feet in the first second of time; if the same body was acted upon in a horizontal direction by an impulse equal to its weight, it would move in that direction the same distance in an equal time; it follows, then, that the water in the trunk will have the effect, proportionable to its weight, of retarding the water from being discharged from the cylinder in too short a time.

Near the cylinder, on the top of the trunk, there is a valve to admit air, which follows the water that is then in motion, and gives time for the water to rise gradually into the trunk through valves, at its bottom, for that purpose; this water has but little motion with respect to the boat, and is therefore capable of resisting the next stroke of the engine.

Rumsey published a pamphlet in Philadelphia, May 7th, 1788, wherein he denounced Fitch in no measured terms—using expressions towards him as plain as to say that he, Fitch, got his idea of a steamboat from a Capt. Bedinger, who described Rumsey's boat to him. Rumsey published a number of affidavits to prove that he was the original inventor of the steamboat, and among the rest a letter from General Washington, to prove that he had spoken to him of employing steam as a prime mover. Fitch's pamphlet is very rare, but there is one in the New-York Society Library, in Vol. 82 of Pamphlets.

Three days after Mr. Rumsey published his pamphlet, John Fitch published an answer to it, which pamphlet, if it came from his pen, gives evidence of a mind skilled in metaphysics, ingenious in detecting the weak points of his opponent's argument, and skilful in making a capital specious plea.—Fitch admits that neither himself nor Rumsey were the first who suggested the idea of propelling vessels by steam, but that he was the first who matured the idea, constructed a model, and made the actual experiment. This was, he says, "about the middle of April, 1785." Rumsey claimed to have matured his plan in 1784.

As the plans of both Rumsey and Fitch were different from those employed at the present day, we have exhibited their inventions, and all that can be justly claimed for them is, that they were modifications of the manner of applying steam to propel boats, but neither Fitch nor Rumsey were the first who actually made the experiments of applying steam power to propel vessels. Fitch undoubtedly thought he was, and said he was, and so did Rumsey, but we have shown that Jonathan Hulls took out a patent for the application of steam to propel boats, forty-eight years before Fitch or Rumsey (by their own admissions) thought upon the subject.

It is needless for us to go into the controversial points of the original merits of these two inventors. We look upon them both as very ingenious men, and Rumsey as possessing as much original genius as Fitch, for he got patents for other inventions beside his steamboat. Rumsey was the original inventor of propelling boats by steam power driving a jet of water out of the stern, and Fitch that of using his very ingenious combination of paddles, and beside he has a good claim to the paddle-wheels. It is stated that John Bernouli, the famous mathematician, suggested the idea (first) of propelling a vessel by the reaction of the water, but we have no evidence that he ever matured his *idea.* Rumsey's claims are not weakened by those of Bernouli. John Fitch claims our deepest sympathies. He was very unfortunate, and terminated his life by poison at Bardstown, Ky., in 1796.

CHAPTER III.

EVANS, SYMINGTON, MILLER.

In 1768, Oliver Evans, of Philadelphia, a man of a most ingenious and constructive turn of mind for mechanics, proposed to navigate vessels by steam and paddle-wheels. About this time a boat was run for a short time, by steam, between Philadelphia and Bordentown, but we have no means of ascertaining the nature and construction of the propelling parts. About the same time Dr. Franklin proposed to propel vessels by the immediate action of the steam upon water, but this was found to be utterly incompetent for the purpose. A Mr. Latrobe, a keen opponent of Evans, but a man celebrated as an engineer, unfortunately for his own future fame, wrote a work against the steam engine for impelling boats. It no doubt at the time retarded steam navigation in America, for, as a general thing, the man who can give a plausible reason against the introduction of a new invention, is held to be a Solomon, while the inventor is too often looked upon either as a knave or an enthusiast. It was the case with the first inventors of the steamboat.

In 1787, a Mr. Patrick Miller, of Dalswinton, in Scotland, took up the subject, and applied steam to propel a double vessel, with a wheel in the stern.

The steam engine for this boat was made and fitted up by a very ingenious mechanic, named William Symington, and it is carefully preserved to the present day. The success of this boat was very gratifying, but it was on a small scale, the cylinder being only four inches in diameter. In 1789, Mr. Symington again, under the direction of Mr. Miller, fitted up an engine on a double boat, sixty feet long. This boat, on the Forth and Clyde Canal, went at the rate of seven miles per hour, and was very promising as an experiment, but unfortunately the boat was too weak for the machinery, which was taken out, and Mr. Miller tried no more experiments. A work published by his son states, that out of his private fortune, Mr. Miller spent no less than $150,000 making experiments, for which he never received in return a single cent. He was a patriot in mechanical science. It has always appeared strange to us how Mr. Miller came to embrace the idea of a double boat instead of a single one, but so far as it regards the successful and direct application of steam to drive a single *paddle-wheel*, the evidence appears to be in favor of his claims, that is, of having put his invention into actual operation. Twelve years after Miller's last experiment, in 1801 and 1802, Symington induced Lord Dundas, a man of mechanical taste and experience, to build a steamboat for dragging vessels on the Forth and Clyde Canal. The engine for this new boat had a cylinder of twenty-two inches diameter, and four feet stroke. This was quite a large vessel, and it took in tow two sloops of 70 tons burden, and moved them with great ease through the canal at the rate of nineteen and a half miles in six hours—three and a half miles per hour. This was a great feat, for the wind blew a strong head breeze all the time. This steamboat was also laid up, because the proprietors of the canal supposed that the undulation of the water by the wheel, would wash away the banks.

It was during the period of the building of this boat of Symington, that he received, as he states, a visit from Robt. Fulton. He politely made himself known, and told Symington that he was going to return to America soon, but could not go away without seeing the steamboat operate, and would be happy to receive any information Mr. Symington chose to communicate, stating at the same time, that however advantageous the steamboat might be to Great Britain, it would be of far greater benefit to America, with her broad, calm, and long rivers. This is direct testimony that Fulton had the steamboat in his mind before, or why should he go from England to Scotland to see this one? Every inventor, when he has any project in his head, likes to see and know about what is doing in the same line, but Symington was first in the field a *bona fide* steamboat builder. At the request of Fulton, Symington fired up and carried his guest four miles along the canal, and returned to the place of starting. Fulton took notes, and was very particular in his examinations. It is very singular that at this time, and for a long time afterwards, it was thought that steamboats were not capable of being employed except in placid waters. It is to be regretted that there was not enterprise enough in all Scotland, at this time, to encourage Symington to make his experiments on the river Clyde. We believe that we are not saying too much, when we attribute the first real practical steamboat to this man. Our reasons are these:—He was very ingenious, and was employed by Mr. Miller on this account, and he was a practical machinist and engineer—he could make and fit an engine as part of his trade, he was a good tradesman, and had an excellent education.

EVANS, COLONEL STEVENS, ROBERT FULTON, HENRY BELL.

It is stated that Oliver Evans published, in 1785, an account of a mode to propel vessels with paddle-wheels, by his high pressure engines; and although Galloway states that "he fully establishes his claim to the first practical steamboat," still we have no correct evidence to establish the truth of this statement. Neither Rumsey nor Fitch mention his claims in their pamphlets; but he was a most ingenious man.

In 1804, Mr. Stevens of Hoboken, New-York, made a number of trips on the North River, with a small boat twenty-five feet long, which was propelled by a wheel at the stern. Mr. Stevens first tried a rotary engine, but it would not answer; and then he tried one like Watt's, which propelled his boat at the rate of four miles an hour; and it even run at the rate of eight miles per hour for a short distance. This boat was kept going for nearly a fortnight, making excursions for a few miles up and down the river. Stevens rendered an important service to the engineering world by his invention of the tubular boiler, which he patented, and which, as a suggestion, at least, has been the means of working wonders ; for, in a boiler six feet long, four feet wide, and two feet deep, he exposed four hundred feet of surface, in the most advantageous manner, to the action of the fire.

Fig. 9. The Clermont.

While Fitch, Oliver Evans, and John Stevens, were prosecuting their experiments in steam engines and steamboats in America, Robert Fulton was in Europe studying and experimenting on the same subject. He left Philadelphia in 1786 and went to London; and in 1793 he communicated with the Earl of Stanhope about steamboats, and he published a very neat work on the subject in 1796. The Earl of Stanhope was a very ingenious nobleman, and proposed to propel the boat by what was called the duck-foot propeller, which was simply a kind of broad blade, that opened when acting against the water, it being pushed behind the boat on a rod, and closed by the action of the water when drawn back. In this same year Fulton went to France, where he brought the subject before the French Directory and the Minister of Marine. He also proposed to build his Nautilus, to "deliver France and the whole world from British oppression." In 1801 he tried his Nautilus at Brest, under the favor of Napoleon, and remained under water for four hours and a half, but he never blew up a single enemy's ship.

It was in France where Fulton was introduced to Mr. Livingston, his countryman, who, in 1803, assisted Fulton to complete a boat of sixty-six feet long, to be propelled with paddle-wheels, on the Seine. From the number of experiments which Fulton had made before, we believe that Mr. Livingston, in all likelihood, made some good suggestions to him in the building of this boat, for this experiment fully established the confidence of both the projectors, and they at once ordered an engine to be built by Bolton and Watt, in England, to be forwarded to New-York, to introduce the steamboat on American waters. Livingston succeeded in getting a patent from New-York, to navigate all its waters by steam, for twenty years. Fulton arrived in New-York in December, 1806, and in 1807 his steamboat, the Clermont, was launched on the East river; and, although in the course of its erection it was called "Fulton's Folly," and he was looked upon as a man beside himself, yet his vessel had not proceeded one hundred yards from the shore, before the incredulous multitude, who had assembled to witness its failure, were convinced of its utility. This vessel made regular trips to Albany, and it may be said, that from the first stroke of her paddles steam navigation has never ceased for a single day. She established regular steam navigation. She made her first trip to Albany in thirty-two hours, being at the rate of five miles per hour. The Clermont was one hundred and sixty tons. The cylinder was twenty-four inches in diameter and four feet stroke. The Clermont, on her first voyage, wonderfully astonished the simple people on the banks of the Hudson. She used dry pine wood for fuel, which sent up a column of flame and smoke above her funnel. Some thought she was a monster fire-eater, coming to warn them of the end of time. Many on board of sloops on the river, were so terrified by the noise of her machinery and paddles, and the lurid glare of her fires at night, that they rushed below decks, to hide from the monster which fed upon fire, and dashed over the water against wind and tide.

Some have endeavored to tarnish the fame of Fulton by endeavoring to rob him of all honor or merit; but he deserves great praise, and his memory will always be respected by every impartial person who looks back upon the works which he accomplished. Up to the period of the Clermont's first trial, we have seen that the subject of steam navigation had been brought before the public at various periods, in different parts of the world, from 1736. The advancements made in the art, may be said to have been gradual; one inventor profiting by the failures of his predecessor; and surely we must give credit to the sagacity that perceives how to remedy a defect. Until James Watt improved the steam engine, and made it double-acting, no steamboat was successful; and when we consider that he built the engine of the Clermont—the first successful boat—we cannot shut our eyes to his merits in connection with improvements in steam navigation.

It very often happens that a good idea is embraced in a new invention—a new principle of action developed; but it also often happens, that there is some great fault in carrying it into execution; we are, somehow or other, very liable to make blunders, and only get our wisdom in a negative manner—dear bought experience; and in the case of steam navigation, the *honest* historian will state facts in such a manner as not to adorn the character of one inventor at the expense of another.

After Fulton's successful experiment in America,.Henry Bell, a self-taught engineer, constructed a boat at his own expense, in 1811. It was ten feet wide and forty feet long, and worked with an engine of three horse power, and with paddle-wheels. This boat was named the *Comet*, and was perfectly successful. The same nautical architect who built her hull, was the gentleman (*John Wood*) who built the hull of the Europa, one of the finest pieces of nautical architecture in the world. So far as it regards paddle-wheels—the propelling devices—Fulton's and Bell's were identical, but from them both, we can trace two distinct kinds of steam vessels. Our marine, or sea steamships, are built upon the basis of Bell's first boat, and our river boats, upon that of Fulton.

In our school libraries there is a book containing a biography of Robert Fulton, wherein it is stated that Henry Bell assisted to put up the machinery of the Clermont, and afterwards went back and established steam navigation in Britain. This is incorrect. Henry Bell was never in America. The mistake is copied from an error in a report of a committee of the House of Commons. We have stated before, that more credit should be awarded to Symington than prevailing history allows to him. Fulton saw his boat in operation, and so did Bell; and Bell took drawings of the machinery and furnished them to Fulton, with whom he was acquainted. Both of these men profited by Symington's skill, and had sagacity to see his defects, and the genius to remedy them. In the arrangement of machinery to effect a new object, it is as essential to apply the same aright, for success, as to plan the application of it to a new object. It is in this capacity that we would give Symington credit, he being a skilful and ingenious practical mechanic.

It is a fault in the character of most inventors, that they claim too much. Both Fulton and Bell believed themselves to be the first real inventors of the steamboat. The honor we would assign them—and it is the greatest we can award to them as inventors—is, they were the first successful steamboat inventors; they established steam navigation; and we cannot sufficiently estimate the importance of their inventions, nor calculate the vast benefits they have conferred upon the human race. Without detracting from the merits of one inventor to garnish the brow of another, we will say, that Robert Fulton was the first who successfully established steam navigation in America, and Henry Bell was the first in Europe.

In 1812, a plan to propel vessels without steam, was projected in New-York, to completely overturn the act of Legislature granted to Fulton, without setting the Hudson river on fire. It annoyed Fulton not a little before it was fairly tried. It was nothing less than to propel the vessel by springs and a pendulum. This boat, the wheels of which revolved with great rapidity when on the stocks, stood *stock* still when she was launched into the water. Robert Fulton died in February, 1815. He was one of Nature's noblemen, in every sense of the word, and the nation felt that she lost one of her great men, when he was laid in the grave.

CHAPTER IV.

BUCHANAN, LINAKER, GORDON, HILL, PALMER, NAIRNE, SKENE.

In Buchanan's work we are told that among the papers of William Linaker, of Portsmouth, England, found after his death, there was described a plan to propel vessels by water, in a different way from that of Rumsey. The steam engine had no piston, but drew the water and expelled it, on the principle of Savery's engine.

After the value of side paddle-wheels had been successfully established, both in America and Europe, various inventors arose to improve them, by forming plans to make the paddles enter and leave the water vertically. It will be observed, as we proceed in this history, that the majority of all the propelling devices, invented since 1811, have this object in view.

The third boat that was built on the Clyde, in Britain, was constructed with paddle-wheels to enter and leave the water vertically. Mr. Robertson Buchanan was the projector—an ingenious, scientific man, and above all, a practical engineer of the first order. His plan was very ingenious, and is thus described:

Fig. 10.

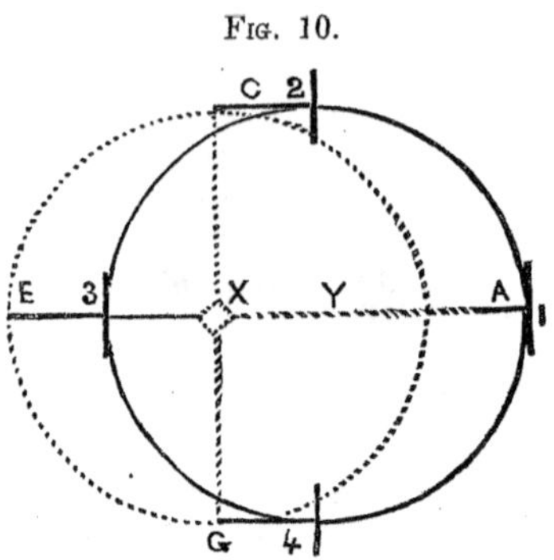

If two equal rings or circular lines in the same plane, or in planes parallel to each other, be conceived to revolve each upon its respective centre, in its own plane, with one and the same uniform velocity, and in the same direction with regard to parts of the rings, or lines alike situated, and any point be taken in one of the lines or rings, and a right line be drawn from that point, parallel to a line supposed to join the centres, until it meets the other ring or circle, then the right line, so drawn, will be equal to the line of distance between the centres, and will continue equal and parallel to that line of distance, during the whole of every revolution so made.

The dotted circle and the black circle in the accompanying figure, denote the rings or circles mentioned in the theorem, and Y and X denote their centres; and the lines 1 A, parallel to an equal to X Y, the line of distance of the centres, will continue equal and parallel to that line of distance, in the positions 2 C, and 3 E, and 4 G, and in all other positions into which the point 1, can be brought, during the uniform, equal and similarly directed revolutions of the two circles.

The amount of friction caused by the eccentric movement was enormous, and the scheme was abandoned.

In 1819, three very scientific gentlemen of Glasgow, Scotland, conceived the idea of propelling vessels by water in a different way from Rumsey or Linaker. The scheme was to discharge water behind with great velocity, from pipes placed under the surface, using the water underneath the surface somewhat as a fulcrum. After an expensive experiment the propelling power was found to be totally inefficient to compete with paddle-wheels, and it was therefore abandoned.

Fig. 11.

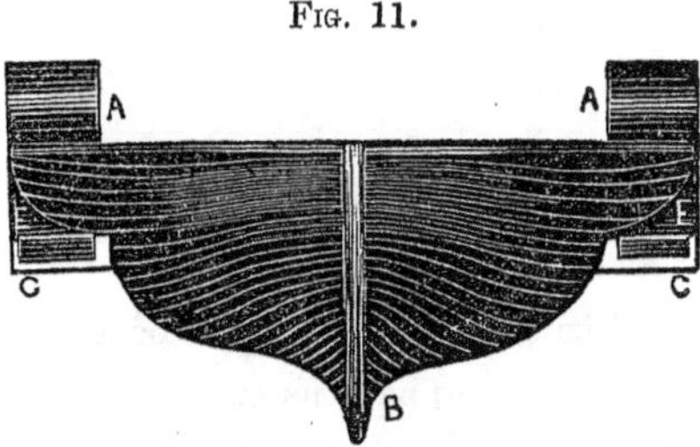

In 1822, a Mr. D. Gordon, of London, invented the casing for the paddles, allowing the water to enter at an aperture below the level of the water line, but allowing the water to leave freely at the back. Figure 11, is a view towards the head of the vessel. A is the paddle-wheel case; B the fore part of the keel, and C the place for the water to enter, below the water line, E. The aperture to admit the water, was furnished with a sluice to admit a greater or less quantity of water, according to the velocity of the vessel or the roughness of the water. This invention was tried—but laid aside.

The first steamboat that was built on the Mississippi was named the "Enterprise," and was about 70 tons burden; she was built with a single wheel placed in her stern, and in 1815, took 28 days to go from New Orleans to Cincinnati. Considering the state of the river at that period, this was not a bad voyage. In 1789, Symington navigated canals with only one paddle-wheel in the stern, but in 1822, Gordon made an improvement, by placing the wheel in the stern as here represented in

Fig. 12.

This is a longitudinal section of the boat, intended to be driven by steam, but no apparatus of that kind shown. It has a channel made through its whole length at the bottom, being open at its under side (like an inverted trough) until it comes to the place where the paddle-wheel case commences, and there the channel is closed up under the paddles, nearly to touch their extremities as they revolve. She was to be steered by two rudders, one on each side of the paddle-wheel, connected together by jointed rods so as to be moved by one tiller. A is the wheel, and C is the entrance for the water coming along the channel spoken of, which then freely escapes behind. The entrance aperture may be furnished with a gate to admit just as much or as little water as is desired, and with a grate in it to prevent sticks, &c., from injuring the paddles. For canals this invention is one of no inconsiderable merit.

Fig. 13.

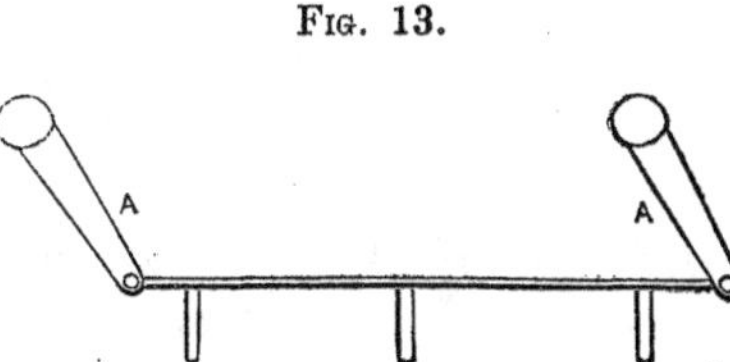

About this period it was also proposed to employ reciprocating paddles as substitute for the paddle-wheel, to enter and leave the water vertically, as herein represented. A A fig. 13, are the cranks which are moved by the engine, and turns with them the horizontal bar to which the vertical paddles are fixed. It is very evident that these paddles cannot be moved fast enough to afford the slightest shadow of a hope in competing with a paddle-wheel, back lift of water and all.

Fig. 14.

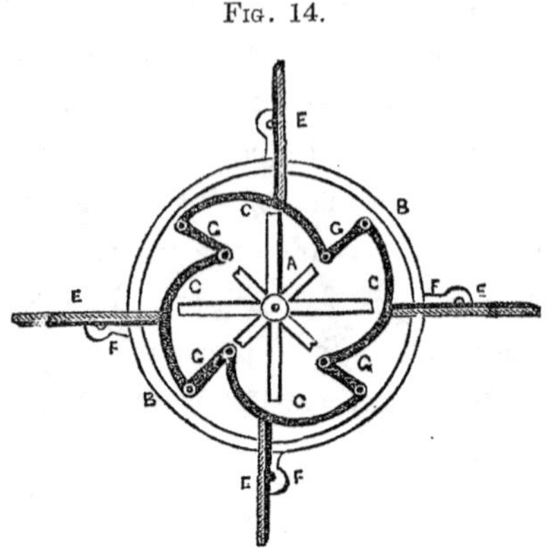

Figures 14, 15 and 16, is another plan that was invented by a Mr. *Hill*, of Woolwich, Eng., to make the paddles enter and leave the water vertically, and to pass through the water elliptically, a hobby indulged in by a great many since that time. This plan, however, is very ingenious, as will be observed by the accompanying description of the separate figures of side views, the same letters referring to like parts:—A A A represent the spokes of the paddle-wheel, shown as disconnected and broken off from the periphery, B B, to prevent its being confused with the novel propelling part; C C C C are four bent levers, one of which is shown separately by fig. 16; E E E E represent the edges of the paddle boards, which are bolted to the straight arms of the levers, C, and are connected by axles to four short arms, F F F F, which radiate from the periphery of the wheel; each end of the curved part of the levers is attached to the next lever in the series, by an intermediate short rod, G G G G. Owing to this mode of connecting the short rods by pivot joints, the

Fig. 15.

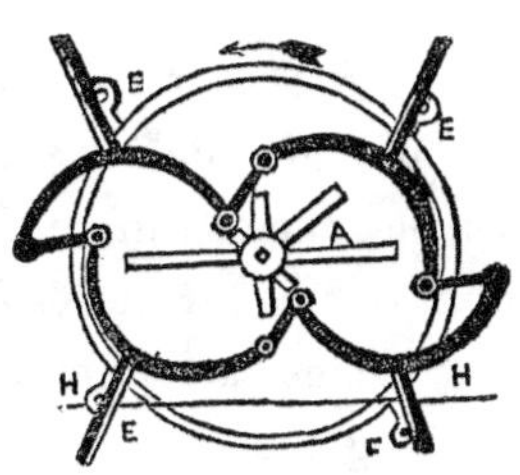

resistance of the water H H against each immersed paddle, causes the next in succession which is entering the water, to be depressed at its extremity, thereby throwing it into that position or that angle with the surface of the water, by which it meets with the least impediment to its immersion. The resistance of the water upon the paddle that has preceded it,

Fig. 16.

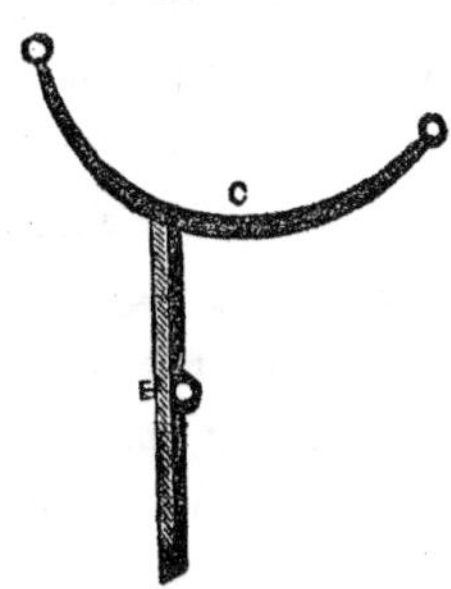

then draws the other into the vertical position, at the same time that it is itself being raised out of the water, at a similar angle to that by which it entered; these motions are communicated successively to all the paddles by the revolution of the wheel.

In the Repertory of Arts there is a description of a patent granted (1826) to a Mr. Palmer, of the Royal Mint, which strongly resembles the one granted to the Engineer of the American Mint, the co-partner of John Fitch. This invention consisted of chains passing horizontally along the sides of a vessel, or along the bottom, between false keels, with paddles jointed to a guide frame to which they are attached in such a manner, that when the chain is drawn in a direction from stem to stern, the paddles will be kept in a perpendicular position by small check chains, proceeding from the lower extremity of the paddle, to the main chain or guide frame, in an angular position; thus forming a resistance to the water, which propels the vessel forward, as the chains with the paddles are dragged backward. When the horizontal parts of the chains are returned, or moved from stern to stem, the paddles fold up and and take a horizontal position with the chains, and therefore form no resistance in passing through the water. The chains are kept in their places by passing over guide pulleys at each end of the horizontal or lower ports, and over wheels at the upper ports. The wheels are furnished with spikes on their peripheries, which take into the links of the chains. These wheels are put in motion by a band passing over a drum in connection with a steam-engine, and round a small rigger attached to the axis of each of the spiked wheels.

If the paddles be used on the sides of the vessel, the spiked wheels and guide pulleys are attached to triangular frames, which are firmly fixed to the sides. But if they be applied to the bottom of the vessel (when they are used for barges on canals, as they will in that case agitate the water less, and consequently do less injury to the banks of the canal), they must be placed between false keels.

The accompanying engraving is a modification of this invention :

Fig. 17.

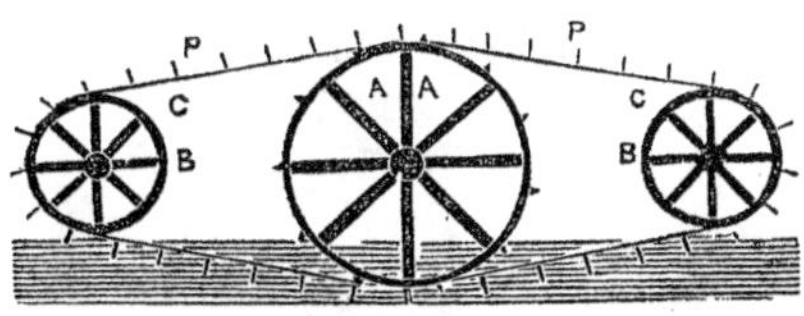

A A is the large wheel or drum, having studs on its circumference to work the chains both above and below. B B two smaller drums, over which the chain passes, which serve to keep it in the proper position, and each of which have raised edges to prevent the chains from slipping off. One of the small drums is made to move by a screw, so as to tighten or slacken the chain when required ; and both may be made to fix either higher or lower, so as to give the paddles a greater or less sweep or stroke of the water. The paddles, chains, drums, and the water line are shown, the small drums being raised above the centre of the large drum. C C are parts of the chain; P P P P the paddle boards.

The next is a very curious contrivance, by a Mr. Nairn, of equal age with the above.

Two, four, or more levers are to be suspended over the sides of a vessel, and to descend nearly as low as the vessel's keel. These levers are to be moved backwards and forwards, like a pendulum, the motion being communicated by a steam engine, or other prime mover; and that the levers may experience but little resistance from the water, they should be of such a shape as to present in their horizontal section a form like the adjoining figure.

Fig. 18.

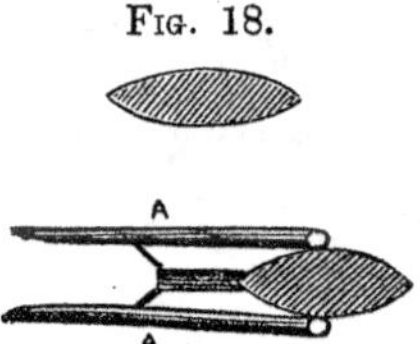

At each side of the lever, at its lower extremity, is attached a broad plate of iron, A A, fig. 18, by means of hinge joints, which, upon the lever being moved forward, close, and offer no resistance; but when it is moved backward, they open or expand, and thereby impel the vessel forward. To prevent their opening beyond the proper angle, which is from 140 to 160 degrees, a circular arc may pass through them, or they may be connected to chains, which only allow them a certain range of opening, or any other method to admit their expansion within due limits.

There have been many previous contrivances for propelling, bearing a resemblance to this, which have failed in practice; and we can discover nothing in the present contrivance calculated to render it an exception. It is just a modification of the duck-foot propeller.

Fig. 19.

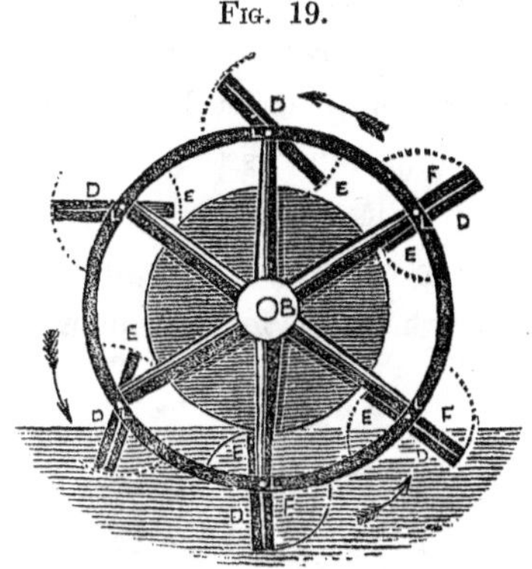

This invention is that of Lieut. Skene, R. N., invented in 1828. The form and full size of the paddles are a parallelogram, 1 foot deep, by 2 feet wide, terminated by a semi-circle of one foot radius. These paddles are not immovably fixed, but vibrate on axes passing through the two opposite annular plates that form the periphery of the wheel, in order to allow of their dipping into the water edgeways, and thereby reducing the resistance of the water to the revolution of the wheel. For this purpose, the lower or semi-circular portion of each paddle is loaded with metal, the superior gravity of which, to that of the upper portion, causes each paddle successively, as it enters the water, to assume the vertical position; and to prevent their turning over, a simple stop is provided (which will presently be explained), so that the full effect of the impelling power of the engine may be given to each paddle at the proper time. To prevent the water from escaping sideways between the arms of the wheel, a large disc or circular plate is fixed against the internal sides of the wheel, and of such diameter as not to come within the range of the paddles as they vibrate on their axes.

The number of paddles to each wheel is to be regulated by the diameter of the wheel; which is, for every foot in diameter, one paddle; therefore, for six-foot wheels, there are to be six paddles.

This figure, 19, represents a side elevation of the wheel, with the paddles viewed edgeways. The arms of the wheel revolve upon the shaft B. D D D are paddles, of which, F F F are the loaded sides; L L are the axes of the paddles, the dotted arcs of circles, at the extremities of the paddles, show the range of their motion, which is arrested by the stops, E, that consist merely of a prolongation of the upper sides of the paddles striking against the arms, or the inside of the rims of the wheel.

Experiments were made with this paddle-wheel, the paddles measuring 16 by 16 inches, and their extremities, describing a circle of nine feet nine inches in diameter. The boat run on the River Thames, the engine making 45 strokes per minute. It was an entire failure, for it went much slower when the paddles operated as designed, than by an experiment of lashing them to make them immovable. The back-water was excessive, thrown right astern. In turning, the paddles seemed to strike the arms and the rim of the wheel with great violence, causing a great noise. The vibration of the vessel was very great, and the paddle-box shook with great violence. In revolving rapidly, it is very evident that the centrifugal force, has a tendency to throw the paddles outward, to prevent them from entering the water in a vertical position; consequently no advantage but a disadvantage would be the result. It is a great evil also to have the lower part of the paddles heavier than the upper, if turning, as these paddles do, on an axis. The reason of this is obvious, not in entering, but in rising out of the water, causing an unequal wear on the axis, thereby creating a great deal of friction. The thicker the blades of the paddles, so much of their useful effect must be subtracted from the circumference of the wheel, when we measure the distance the vessel travels, by the number of revolutions of the wheel.

CHAPTER V.

PAUL STEENSTRUP'S PADDLE-WHEELS.

THE form and full size of the paddle-wheels are a parallelogram, 1 foot deep, by 2 feet wide, terminated by a semicircle of 1 foot radius. These paddles are not immovably fixed, but turn on axes passing through the two opposite annular plates that form the periphery of the wheel, in order to allow of their dipping into the water edgeways, and thereby reduce the resistance of the water to the revolution of the wheel.

FIG. 20.

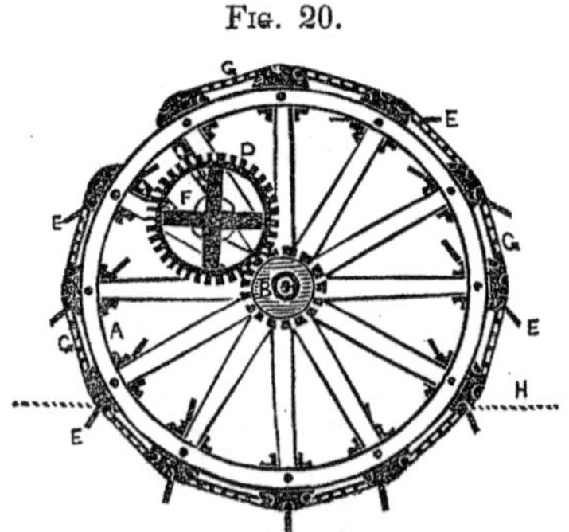

This figure, 20, represents a side elevation of the wheel, with the paddles viewed edgeways.

A represents the paddle-wheel, B a cog-wheel bolted to the vessel's side, concentric with A and allowing the shaft C of the paddle-wheel to revolve in its centre; D a cog-wheel, double the diameter of B, revolving upon an axis supported by the arms of the paddle-wheel, and gearing into B; E the paddle, suspended by axles turning in the rim of the wheel: on each of these axles is fixed a chain wheel F, and a similar wheel is fixed on the axis of the cog-wheel D; G is an endless chain, passing over the wheels, on the periphery of the paddle-wheel, and under the wheel F, on the axis of D; H represents a water-line.

It will now be perceived that when the paddle-wheel is set in motion, the toothed wheel B being fixed, causes the large-toothed wheel D, to revolve upon its own centre, at the same time that it is carried round by the paddle-wheel, in a manner similar to the sun and planet wheel, in Watt's steam engine. The wheel D, being double the diameter of B, will perform one revolution upon its own axis, in the same time that it is carried round once by the paddle-wheel; and by means of the endless chain, passing under the small wheel F, on its axis, will cause each paddle to revolve once on its axis in the same time; and each paddle is constantly directed to the highest point in the rim of the wheel.

This wheel was patented as far back as 1828, and its very complexity is enough to condemn it at a glance. It is a most astonishing thing, how some people to remedy an evil, adopt another of far greater magnitude. For complexity and impracticability, it was an ingenious invention: and, if these are qualities to recommend any thing, it surely deserves the highest eulogiums.

TRIPLE CRANK PROPELLER.

This is a plan of propellers which, when it was brought forward by its inventor, a Mr. Stevens, in 1828, it was somewhat highly flattered. Like all other improvements to supersede the common paddle-wheel, its object was to allow the paddle to enter the water vertically and rise out of it in the same way, so as to prevent jarring in the first case, and water lift in the other—two evils attributed to the common paddle-wheel, but greatly magnified.

In this engraving, Fig. 21, we have a side elevation of the machinery in the paddle-box, which is placed on the vessel in the common way. A series of paddles are attached to a three-throw crank, and by means of radius and guiding rods, the paddles are made to describe the segment of an ellipsis in the water.

Each throw of the crank revolves between two parallel bars, with its bearings upon them, and carrying with them a set of paddles (the bars are not seen). There are thus four bearings, the innermost of which it fixed to the vessel's side and the outer one on the frame of the paddle-box. The circle of motion described by the triple crank being equally divided (120 degrees apart) between each throw, and thus balance one another on their general axis. This invention was fairly tested by a number of experiments, but failed to rival the old paddle-wheel. It has been revived a great number of times since the above date.

Fig. 21.

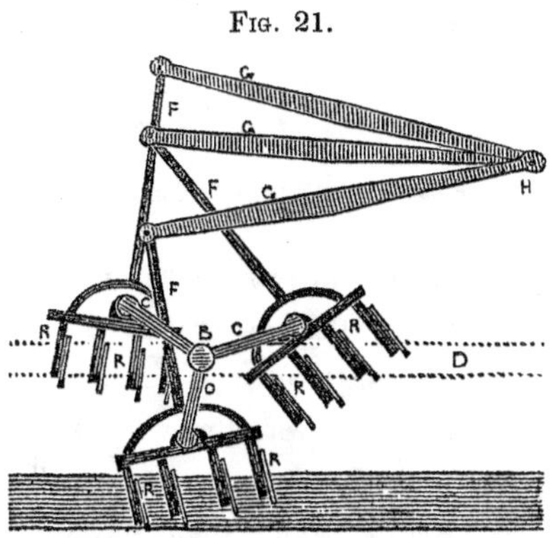

There is a centre to the axis of the cranks C C C, and B is one of its bearings, supported on the side frame of the paddle-box; D D (represented by two dotted horrizontal lines,) is one of the longitudinal beams which support the other bearings of the said axis; and the extremities of D D are transverse to support them. In the paddle-box, provision is made for the occasional rise of the rods G and F, if it be not thought desirable to carry the paddle-box above them; R R are three sets of paddles, each set being carried by a division of the triple crank, which revolves between, and has its bearings upon parallel bars; the paddles are directed in their appropriate motion by means of the guide rods F F F, and the radius rods G G G, the latter of which work on a fixed beam or centre at H; there are arched spreaders, to keep the paddles steady and firm; the paddles are marked R and are fixed to vertical bars in the ordinary way; the upper ends of the bars being inserted in sockets cast in the paddle carriage.

SIDE FAN PROPELLER.

Various plans have been proposed from time to time, to propel by a kind of propeller that would close when moving forward against the water, to offer at least but little resistance to it, and would open when moving backward, to act with great surface and power on the water. The duck-foot Propeller, of the Earl of Stanhope, was devised to act on this principle, which really has something very plausible and self-commending in it. As practical experiment, however, is the real test of any invention—the touchstone of its economical value—so in the case of the duck-foot paddle, it was "weighed in the balance and found wanting."

Fig. 22.

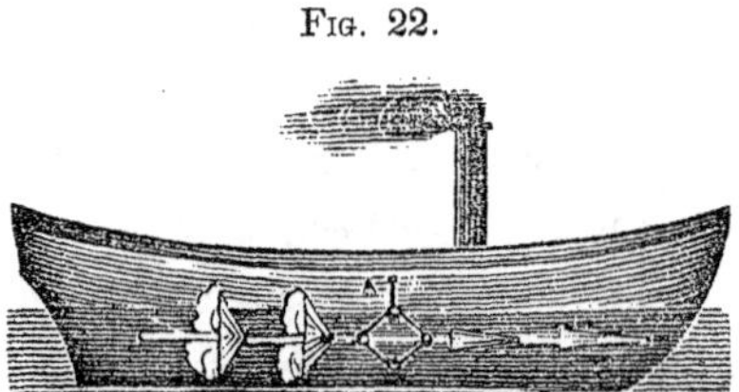

The invention represented in this engraving, Fig. 22, was invented about twenty years ago, and it was the result of observing the powerful action of the "tail of a fish." The piston of the engine being attached to the rod, A, will alternately open and shut a series of sliding sub-marine fans, which may be variously constructed, and placed without the sides or bow, or stern of a vessel, keeping up a constant pressure upon the water, and a consequent motion upon the vessel forward, without backwater or splashing. Hinged paddles attached to a reciprocating frame, so as to fold upwards, and assume a horizontal position when moving forwards, and to have their flat full surfaces acting upon the water when moving backwards, have been brought forward oftentimes since the above was brought forward. About two years ago, only, the same thing was brought forward in New York, and high hopes were entertained about it, but it now reposes in oblivion.

It is something very annoying to the man accustomed to scientific research, to find the same things invented over and over again by different individuals, living in different places. Within three years the duck-foot propeller has appeared in public print, as something new, because somewhat modified from the original one, in contour and arrangement. In the London Mechanics Magazine, for 1845, there are two engravings of plans for propelling, by applying the direct action of the piston rod to move a fan piston to act upon the water at the stern of a vessel, and close when moving forward, so as to propel the vessel upon the same principle as that represented above. There can be no question of its simplicity, but simplicity, although desirable, is not always possible, to accomplish certain objects. Everything must be judged by its effects—its whole effects.

GALLOWAY'S PADDLE-WHEEL.

Almost every person has heard of "Morgan's Paddle-Wheel;" the honor of the invention belongs to Elijah Galloway, the author of a very valuable history of the "Steam Engine." The object of Galloway's invention was like that of many others, viz., to provide a remedy for the loss of power and other inconveniences arising from the oblique position in which the paddles enter and leave the water.

Fig. 23.

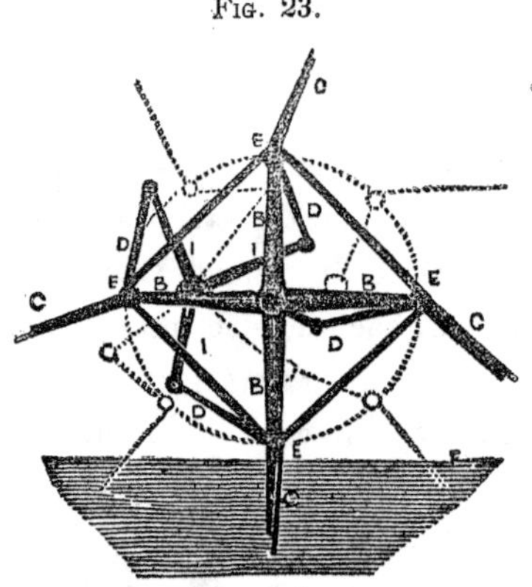

This engraving represents his invention, for which a patent was secured in 1829. Each paddle turns on an axis through the medium of projecting levers, firmly fixed to the paddles at their axis of motion, and connecting rods proceeding from these levers to the extremity of a fixed crank, adjustable at a given distance from the centre of motion of the paddle-wheel, which consists of four radiating arms connected at their extremities by strengthening braces.

B B, Fig. 23, represents four arms radiating from a central axis, the extremities of which E E, are connected by bracing rods from one to the other. C C, are the paddles, firmly fixed to which are the levers, D D, forming angles of about 120 degrees to each other, and turning together on axes at E E; F, represents the water-line. There is a crank, fixed centrally to the axis of the wheel, but so as not to revolve with it; this crank is alterable at pleasure by means of a set screw, which causes the paddles, through the medium of the connecting rods I I I, to take such an angle with the water line, as may be deemed most desirable for propelling; the rods I, however, are connected to a revolving collar on the crank, which allows of their free rotary motion, while it draws the paddles uniformly into the positions shown in the engraving, when the arm of the crank is set in a horizontal position, as represented. The dotted lines show the position the paddles assume in the intermediate parts of their revolution, or the relative position they would take, if there were eight paddles attached to the wheel.

Fig. 24.

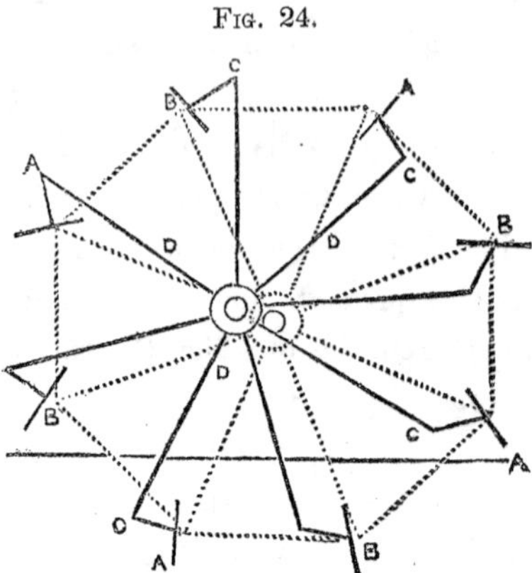

This figure represents the mechanism of Morgan's wheel; A A A A, &c., are the paddles which turn upon spindles, having a bearing in the angles of the framework of the wheel, B B B, and which is of a polygonal figure, with as many sides as it is required to have paddles. The inside frame or polygon is alone attached to the shaft of the engine, which does not continue beyond the side of the vessel; and the outer one has an independent bearing on a centre attached to the paddle box, so that it receives its motion entirely from the rim or angles of the polygon; by this means the space between the sides of the wheel is left entirely free. The part of the shaft or centre upon which the outer side of the wheel revolves, is projected in an inclined direction to the middle between the sides, but of course to a point considerably eccentric with the wheel.

Each paddle has a crank, C, attached to it at an angle of nearly ninety degrees, and rods, D D D, &c., connect the extremity of this crank with a movable boss which revolves upon the fixed eccentric point of the shaft.

It will thus be seen, that in consequence of the fixed point being situated out of the centre, the paddle will assume different positions during the revolution of the wheel, which positions can be so arranged as to differ very little from a vertical direction while passing the lower part of the revolution, or that part where the action of the paddle takes place.

The difference between the "Galloway Paddle-Wheel," and the "Morgan Wheel," consists in one simple point, viz., the axis of the paddles above pass through their ends; in Morgan's the axis passes through the middle of the float. These wheels have been too highly extolled, in our opinion. They are complicated in comparison with the common wheel, and must be far more expensive to keep in repair. Seven vessels in the British Navy have been fitted with these kind of wheels, and some of the steam packets that run on the French coast. The speed of the Firebrand and Flamer, fitted with "Morgan's Wheels," averages only 10.55 miles per hour. If there were any superior benefits to be derived from this kind of wheel, we would expect that they would have been placed in the most superior new British steamships of the Liverpool and North American Line.

The accompanying engraving (Fig. 25.) represents a

plan for making the paddles enter and leave the water in a vertical position by an extra eccentric wheel moving the paddles on their axis—the axis of them passing through their centre. We are not able to tell the inventor's name, we believe, however, that it is "*Poole*;" but the invention is at least twenty years old. A B C D E F are the paddles, which turn round upon their axis as the large wheel to which they are applied revolves. H H H H H are the rods to the two sides of the wheel. I I I I are the concentric rings, with an opening or groove between them, which forms the path for the crank arms, K K K K, to move in.—The centre of the guide rings being eccentric to that of the wheel, causes the paddles to assume the positions represented in the engraving, which were found to be best adapted to the motion of the vessel. The paddle C is supposed to be just dipping into the water, while D is deeply immersed, and E just rising out of it.

Fig. 25.

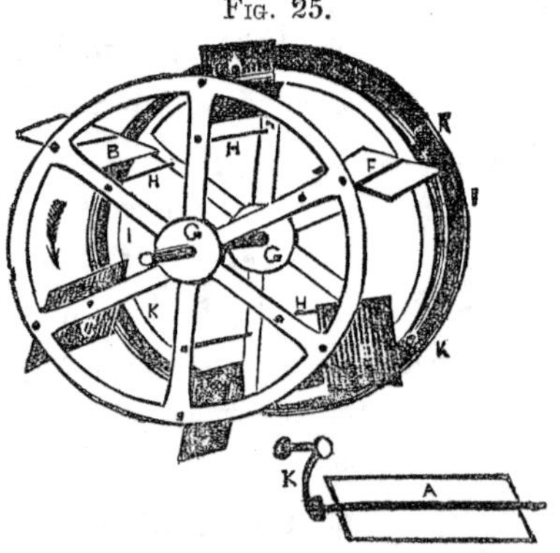

The small figure below the wheel is an underside perspective view of a paddle separately; K is the crank arm connected at one end to the axis, A, and at the other to the anti-friction roller before mentioned, which travels in the groove of the railway.

We have seen no less than three separate re-inventions of this paddle-wheel, within two years. Two of these were invented by men who constructed models and brought them to New-York, the one from St. Louis, the other from Connecticut. The other was a drawing only, made by a gentleman in New-York. Had these gentlemen been acquainted with the above invention, it would have saved them much labor, study, and, consequently, expense. But what is stranger than all this, and what we would not have expected, we are informed that Mr. David Napier, of London, a first rate and one of the most experienced marine engineers in the world, constructed a steamer with wheels like the above, in 1848. His steamboat exhibited astonishing speed, surpassing every steamboat on the Thames, but this might have been owing to some other thing than the paddle-wheels, perhaps the engines, or build of the vessel. At any rate, its superior speed lasted only a few weeks, when, from the number of breakages, she had to be laid aside. Economy embraces, not the speed of a trip, but the number of trips in a given time, performed at the least expense.

The great duty that we wish to perform, is to show what has been already invented, to prevent others from spending their time and money on the like projects.

HEILBRON'S PADDLE-WHEEL.

More than one plan of different motion, has been devised to make the paddles enter and leave the water in a vertical position. One plan is to make the upper and lower edges change position, and enter the water at a different angle. Another is to turn the side edges, or feather the paddles, which will produce the same effect, but requires a different arrangement of machinery. The plan presented here was the invention of Adolph Heilbron of New-York, and was patented in 1829. A revolving motion is given to the paddles, by which they dip into and leave the water as represented in figure 26. The buckets are each fixed upon an arm, which radiates from the centre of the wheel.

Fig. 26.

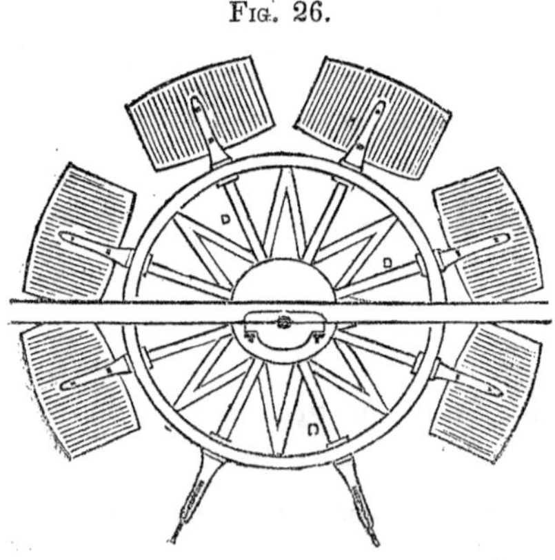

In a wheel so constructed, the paddles may be made to enter the water edgewise, and be turned so as to act upon it at any point which may be preferred. The paddles which are out of the water are all feathered, or turned edgewise, so as to experience but little resistance from the wind, and to require a very shallow box or casing to protect them on each side of the boat. A wheel of this description may be immersed in water to any depth which may be required, or it may be entirely under water, where the depth is sufficient: should such a mode of fixing it be thought advisable, the progress of the boat will be but little impeded thereby.

One great advantage anticipated from these paddles is, the avoiding of those numerous and perpetual concussions produced by the striking of the water by the ordinary floats, which causes a continued, distressing, and very injurious tremulous motion. They enter by their edges, and are gradually brought into action.

Fig. 27.

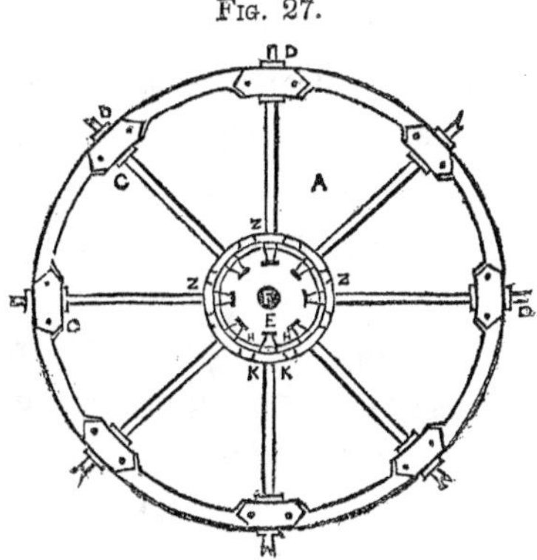

Figure 26, represents one of the said wheels of eight arms or paddles, as it appears when in a finished state, and as applied to the side of a vessel; and figure 27 is a view, on a larger scale, or the central part of the said wheel, as seen from the opposite side, or that nearest to the vessel, for the purpose of showing how the paddle-arms are held and supported in their places, and yet permitted to turn or feather at the proper instant, while the whole wheel turns round. In these several figures, A—is a circular disc or plate of cast iron, having a rim or ring, rising on one side to a sufficient height to give strength and solidity to the said circular plate, and also to hold the boxes C C C, through which the paddle-arms or axis, D D D D, are permitted to turn. The central block of metal E, may be cast in one piece with the disc or plate, but will be better detached, and afterwards fixed to it by screw-bolts. The disc or plate, A A—with its centre block E, forms the central part of the paddle-wheel, which must be firmly keyed, or otherwise fixed upon the main shaft, F, which derives its rotary motion from any power applied within the vessel, and this shaft also passes freely through the centre of a metal wiper carriage, which is firmly and immovably fixed to the side of the vessel, for the purpose of operating upon the wipers or projections H H, of the paddle axis in order to produce the feathering of the paddles. To effect this, the outer face of the wiper carriage presents two annular surfaces, or eccentric grooves, or one will answer to make the paddles turn or feather.

The wipers or projections on the axis of these paddles,

are projections of metal, crossing each other so as to project at right angles from the axis of the paddles, and as these wipers come into contact with one or other of the annular surfaces, the several paddle axes will each make a quarter turn or revolution. Thus the wipers, Z Z, lie with their flat surfaces upon one annular surface of the wiper carriages, and the inner annular surface then presents itself, and acts upon the wipers to turn them round; consequently, the inner wipers will now assume the flat position, and will continue in it, until they are again brought by the motion of the wheel, into contact with the ends of the outer annular surface.

PERKINS' PADDLES.

This propeller, fig. 28, is the invention of the celebrated Jacob Perkins. Each of the paddles is placed on the extremity of a radiating arm, in such a position that its plane, if produced towards the centre of motion, would make with the axis of the paddle-wheel an angle of 45 degrees. The axes of the paddle-wheels are not carried across the vessel in the customary manner, but are carried in a direction sloping towards the stern, and they meet at a point in a straight line, drawn from stem to stern along the middle of the vessel, making with it an angle of 45 degrees, and with each other an angle of 90 degrees. On the extremities of the axis are fixed bevel wheels, which act upon each other, or are both acted upon by an intermediate bevel-wheel in connection with the steam engine, or first mover.

Fig. 28.

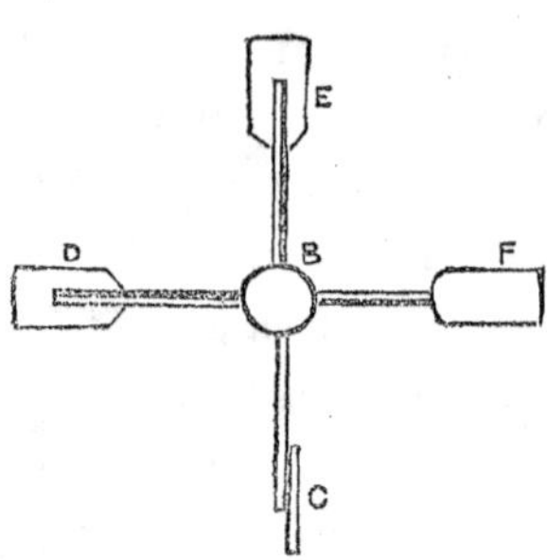

By this arrangement the surface of each paddle, when immersed in the water at its greatest depth, is perpendicular to the side of the vessel, or to the line of motion, as represented at C, fig. 28; at their greatest elevation, each paddle is parallel to the line of motion, as at E; and, when in the horizontal position, whether ascending or descending, the paddle presents an angle of 45 degrees; and from this angle it deviates but little, when in the act of entering or leaving the water, as the inventor purposed to immerse the wheel to about one fourth of its diameter.

Fig. 29 represents the outline (in plan) of a vessel with these paddles attached. A is the boat; B B the paddle axles, to which a uniform motion is given by the engine, through the medium of the bevel gear which connects them: C C are two of the paddles immersed in the water, and in the act of propelling; D D, E E, and F F, are those paddles which succeed each other in the revolution. The oblique action of the blades of the paddles, as they perform their revolutions, will be understood by reference to fig. 28, wherein the paddles are marked by the same letters as in fig. 29.

Fig. 29.

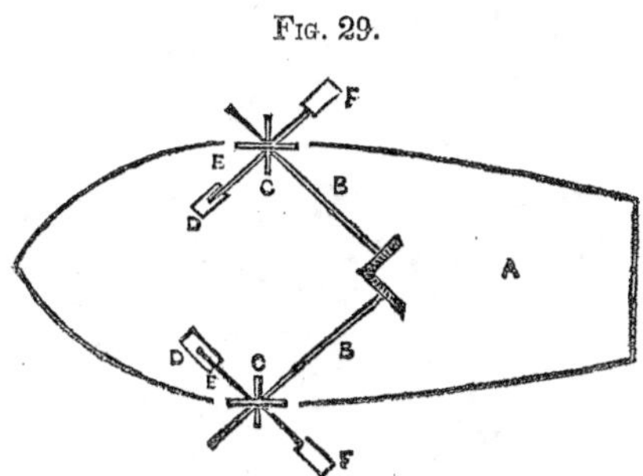

This was invented in 1829, and some experiments made with them were reported in the Journal of the Franklin Institute, with the following very flattering remarks, in comparison with the old paddles: "The saving of fuel appears to be upwards of three in five, and an increase of fifteen per cent. of speed." The article was furnished for the Journal, Vol. IX., by a gentleman in London. It is an inflated piece of commendation on Mr. Perkins's invention, and deals in some severe remarks on the inferiority of the old paddles. Although it was stated how superior this method of propelling was to the paddle-wheels, yet it had its day. It came, and is gone.

HALE'S HORIZONTAL PROPELLER.

Fig. 30.

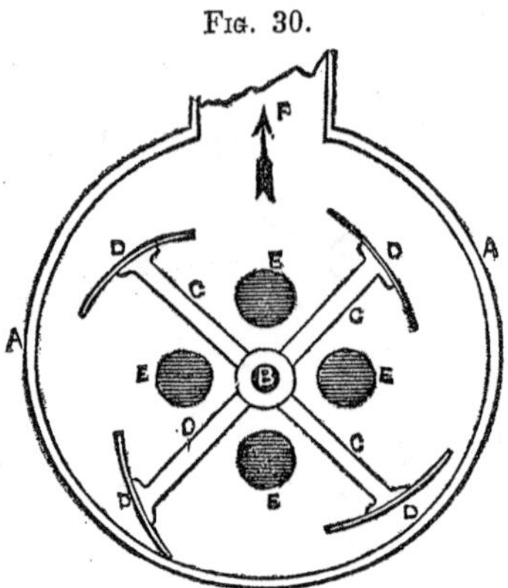

This is a mode of propelling, invented in England, about 1829 or 1830, by a Mr. Hale. It was revived in 1847, by Simpson, and tried both on the Thames and the Clyde. An engraving of it appeared in the Illustrated London News, in 1848; and although it was a little different from Mr. Hale's plan, the principle in no respect was changed; it was only a modification (if it can be called that) of the blower substituted for the paddle-wheel. It received high commendations from some of the foreign periodicals. When employed by Simpson, the boat to which it was applied, with four feet paddle-boxes, went at the rate of eleven miles per hour on the Thames. Its first performance seems to have been its last, for since that period it has not, so far as we are informed, broken the waters of the classic "Clutha," or muddy Thames.

Fig. 30 represents one modification of the apparatus, and consists of an air-tight circular casing A A, containing four arms C C C C, which revolve horizontally on a vertical axis B, placed eccentrically with respect to the casing; at the extremities of the arms are fixed four curved vanes or paddles D D D D, inclined in the manner represented in the drawing. The water enters the casing through the holes E E E, and is expelled by the revolution of the paddles through the opening F, against the external water at the stern, which of course impels the vessel in a contrary direction.

Fig. 31.

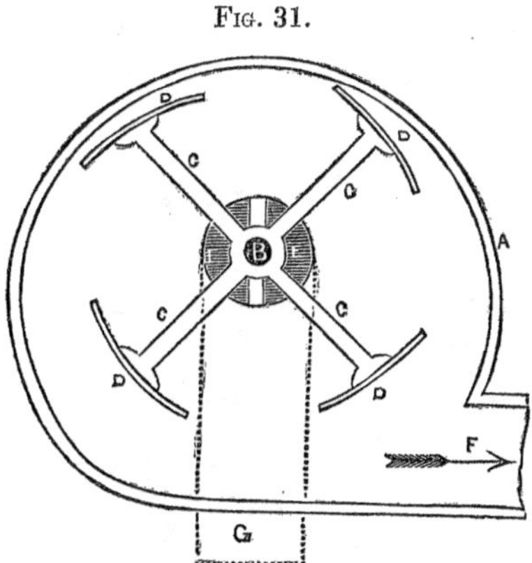

Fig. 31 is another modification of the apparatus. In this similar letters of reference indicate similar parts, with only these differences in the arrangement, that the water is received at one large aperture in the centre of the vanes, the line of direction of the discharge being a tangent to the circle. The dotted lines at G denote a tube leading from the bottom of the vessel, through which the water ascends into the paddle-box; and it may be supposed that similar tubes are employed in the first described plan, for conducting the water into the paddle-box.

The centrifugal force of the paddles acting on the water within the box, produces a pressure all round the interior of the box, which gives a tendency to move in a direction opposite to the side where the opening is made in the circumference; while the same causes accelerate the entrance of the water into the box, which is produced in the first instance by the paddle-box being placed within the vessel, and lower than the exterior water.

FLAP PROPELLER.

Fig. 32.

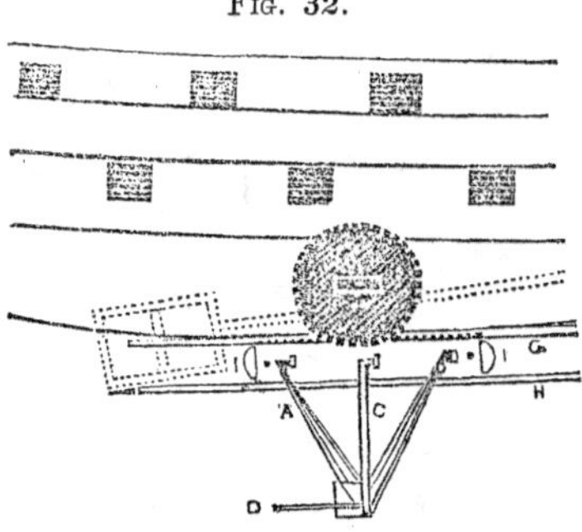

Fig. 32 represents a plan of folding paddles, D, placed on both sides of the vessel. The paddles are attached to hinged joints, A, and to the prolonged axis, C, of the traversing frame. They fold, and present only their sharp edges to the water when moving forward from stern to stem, and they open and act with a large surface on the water when moving backwards. The traversing frames are kept to the sides of the vessel by grooved guides, G, H. I I are friction rollers at the ends, and at the middle, to keep them steady, and to assist them in moving. The upper part of the frame consists of a rack, which is acted upon by the toothed wheel, the axis of which passes through the vessel and terminates in similar wheels on the other side, to act upon similar racks.

To the piston rod of the steam engine, whose cylinder (which may be either situated above or below the plane of the axis) is placed in a position somewhat inclined, as represented by dots, is attached a rod which passes under a pinion on the axis of one pair of the wheels, and over a pinion on the axis of the other pair of wheels, and vice versa; the parts of the rod passing under the one and over the other of these pinions, and thus, by the alternating motion of the piston of the engine, cause one pair of the paddles to move forwards, while the other pair are moving backwards, by which one pair of the paddles on each side are kept continually in action. The paddle stems or axis are attached by stop hinges to the upper part of the paddle frames, and to the lower parts by screw bolts, to fix them when in use. By this arrangement the paddles can be unshipped, and removed from the side of the vessel, whenever the state of the wind renders their application unnecessary.

Fig. 33.

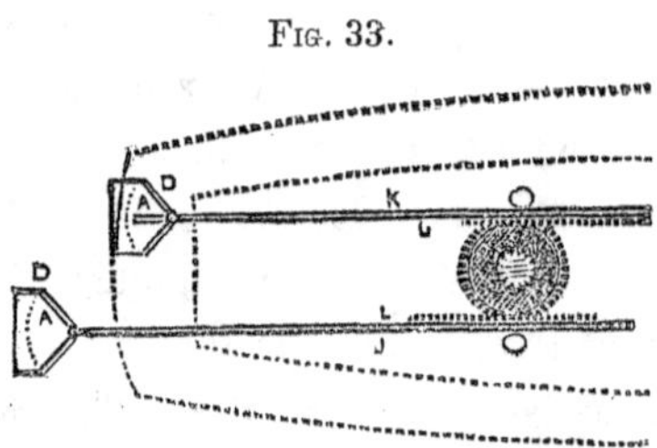

Fig. 33 is another method of attaching similar folding paddles, A D, to the ends of two or more rods projecting through stuffing boxes, under the water line, in the stern of the vessel. These projecting rods, represented by K L, made of metal, and turned cylindrical, are connected with the piston of a steam engine, through racks and pinions, in a manner similar to the connection of the paddle frames before described. The intention of the wheel and pinion, the former acting on the rack connected with the projecting rods, and the latter being acted upon by the rack connected with the engine piston, becomes necessary, to obtain a greater velocity in the paddle than could be given to the piston of a steam engine. The projecting rods have rule joints at the extremities nearest the vessel. When one of the screw bolts is withdrawn, and the rods being detached from the rack, then pushed out beyond the usual extent, and the end to which the paddle is attached elevated to admit of the paddle being easily detached, the rod is to be let down and withdrawn, till it is all within the vessel except its end, which must be left in the hole, or stuffing-box, to prevent leakage; so that with its application there need be no exterior appendages, except when the paddles are in action. This invention is thirty years old, and was patented by a Mr. John Melville.

THE WINGED BOAT.

FIG. 34.

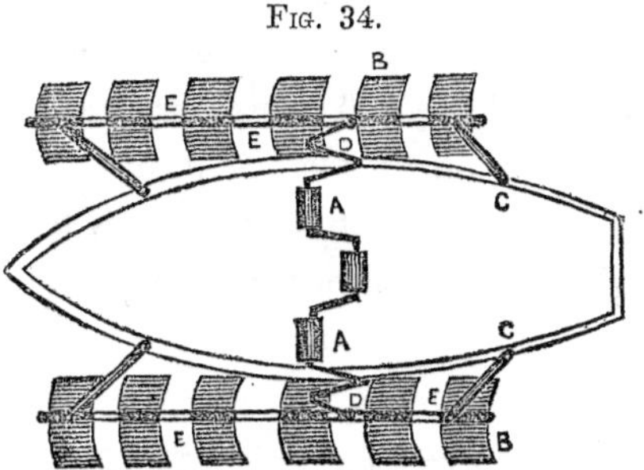

Some of the most extraordinary inventions have burst upon the world, astonishing nobody but their projectors, except it may be surprise at their futility, instead of utility. One man imagines that the wings of birds are the grand subjects for copying after, in works of art, to propel balloons; and another, the fins or tails of *fishes* are the true forms to copy after, for propellers in water. But balloons are not eagles, neither are steamboats sharks, whales, or dolphins. Who would have thought, however, that wings were the best appendages for a steamboat, because they are the best for aerial locomotion? Nevertheless, here we have them. The invention is now thirty years old, and does credit to the name of Mr. Dixon Vallans, of Scotland.

A A is the crank; B B are the wings; C C are the arms, which have moving joints; D D are the shafts, which give motion from the crank to the wings; E E E E are the leaves or feathers of the wings, which, by the forward motion of the crank, fold nearly close to the wing; and by the backward motion fold back, and form a strong pressure against the water; and by that means impel the boat forward with great velocity. The feathers may be either of hard wood or sheet iron, six or eight inches broad, and one foot six inches or two feet long, or they may be made any size, according to the size of the vessel.

Fig. 35.

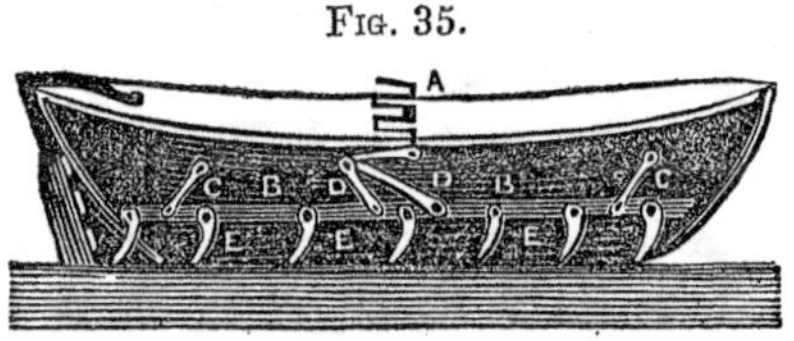

Fig. 34 is a plan view. Fig. 35 is a side view. The same letters refer to like parts. When this invention was first brought out, it was to make a boat run three times faster than with paddle-wheels; but it never did it. It affords a useful lesson for others, and not a small number either, for inventions for the same purpose, less plausible than this, have been brought forward frequently since the above was first brought into notice.

THE INCLINED PLANE STEAMBOAT.

Fig. 36.

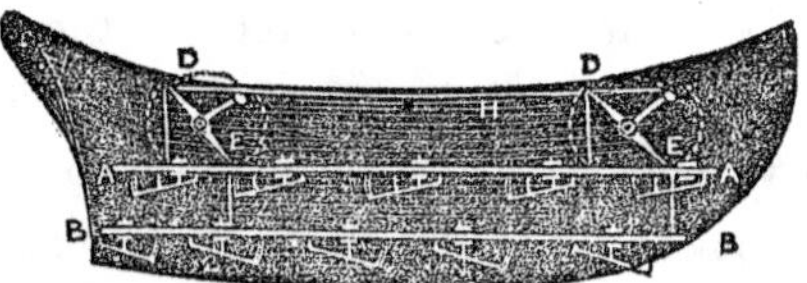

This boat has novelty, but greatly lacks the grand essential, practicability. It is twenty-four years old, and is the invention of Mr. Thomson, of Scotland.

A A and B B are two parallel iron bars, to which the planes are fixed, the one being close to the side of the boat and the other farther off, so that in working alternately up and down, they pass each other freely. These planes projecting from the vessel's sides will be objected to, but as this was merely a trial, improvements, of course, were to follow. 2, 2, &c., the planes, each of which are fastened to the parallel bar, by their respective swivels. D D and E E are working beams that raise and depress the planes. The ends D and D, working close to the boat, for the bar A A, while the other end reaches out for B B; the rod, H, connects two working beams in the manner represented in the figure, so that both ends of the parallel bars, by this communication, rise and sink alike. There are two rocking beams that run across the boat to the other side, where there is the same machinery as on this side, only there is no occasion for more than one connecting rod, H, as this one is sufficient for all. Now, the piston rod of the engine, by working a lever upon one of the rocking cross beams, sets the whole in motion; there was no occasion even for a single wheel or crank; a few connecting rods and levers were all that was required.

The above inclined plane paddles are totally unfit for propelling; they never would answer for a steamboat navigating the ocean. No propeller will answer the purpose, however scientific the ideas embraced in its construction, if it is not perfectly and firmly built in all its parts, without hinges, and such like things.

Fig. 37.

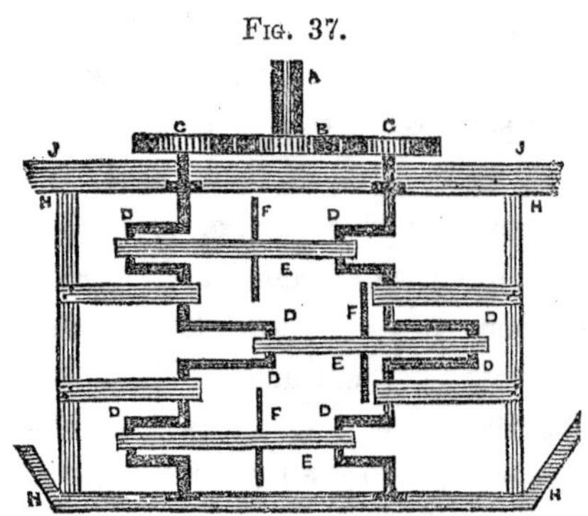

TRIPLE CRANK PROPELLER.

This invention, fig. 37, is like the majority of others, for making the paddles enter and leave the water vertically. The defect of the old revolving paddle-wheel was described

by the inventor, a Mr. Thos. Clark, to be something far superior to the paddle-wheel. A frame is erected on the side of the vessel, and A is the main shaft, on the end of which is the cog-wheel, B, meshing it into the two cog-wheels C C, to give motion to the two shafts having triple cranks, D D D, on each. The crank shafts are secured in the frame, J H, and revolve in proper bearings in the same. E E E are reciprocating bars secured on the extremities of the cranks of both shafts together. The paddles or blades, F F F, are secured on these reciprocating bars. The reciprocating bars E E E, are secured on the cranks to work on them like centres, therefore when the crank shafts revolve, the paddles will receive a reciprocating motion, entering and leaving the water in a very good position, acting upon the water very effectually. The cranks are inclined to one another at equal angles, and the connecting bars preserve the cranks parallel to one another.

We saw a model of this very same description, about five years ago, made by a mechanic in this State, and it was tried at Whitehall, on Lake Chaplain, with flattering hopes. It is twenty-five years, however, since it was first invented. Paddle-wheels can be built stronger and work with less friction than these cranks, but although this is all, it is a great deal, for the compact wheel, every part of which is trussed and arched, has wonderful advantages.

CHAPTER VI.

MR. EWBANK'S (COMMISSIONER OF PATENTS) EXPERIMENTS.

Fig. 38.

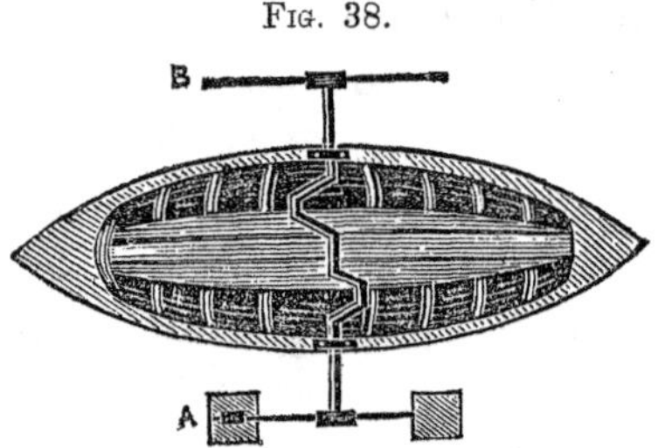

Since part of the Report of the Commissioner of Patents was published, that part of it which relates to the "propulsion of steamers" has been visited by the most scourging criticism of "heroes great and heroes small."

Fig. 39.

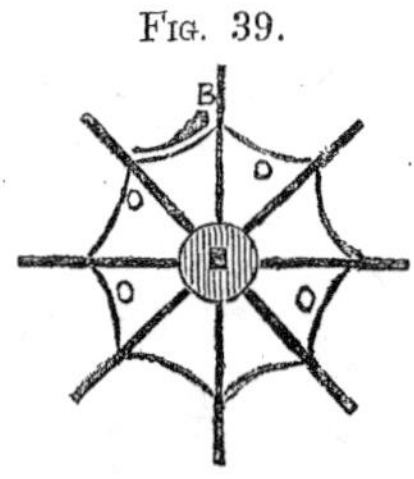

The experiments referred to, were conducted on Harlem River, New-York, in 1845 and 1848.

"For this purpose, the boat, fig. 38, was employed. It was 12½ feet long, and 3½ feet across the middle. A wrought iron shaft, 1 inch square, with a crank, extended across the gunwales, and turned in bearings bolted to them. Each end of the shaft stretched 14 inches over the side of the boat, which prevented the wheels, that were secured on each extremity, from throwing as much water into the vessel as if they had been nearer; and afforded a better opportunity of observing the action of the blades. A person seated at one end of the boat, readily turned the wheels in either direction, by alternately pushing from and pulling towards him, two upright rods, which moved in joints at the bottom of the boat, and were connected to the cranks by horizontal rods or pitmen.

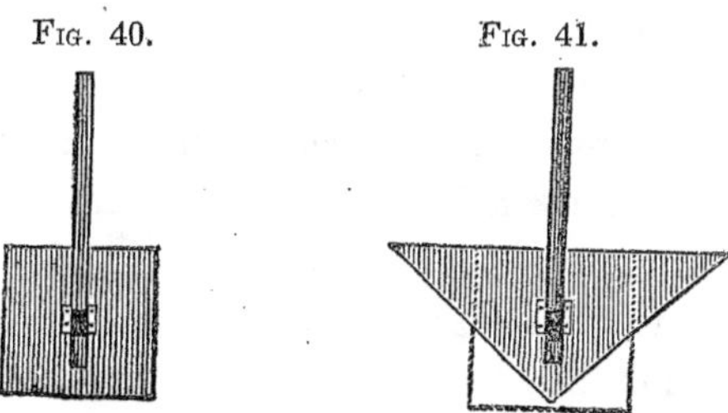
Fig. 40. Fig. 41.

The wheels were very light, and of the simplest construction. One is figured at B. Eight slender arms, of 5-16 square iron, with their inner ends cast in the central piece, extended 20 inches from the centre, and thus made a 40-inch wheel. To stiffen them, and transmit any strain upon one to the whole, they were braced tightly together by the wire, O O O, fig. 39, which was wound round each arm, and retained by slight notches at the corners. The various blades or paddles were cut out of stout sheet iron. Square sockets, to slide over the arms, were riveted to the paddles, by which means they were readily adjusted and secured at uniform distance from the axes. All were of the same area—49 inches.

To test the qualities of the boat, and get her into working trim, blades, 7 inches square, fig. 40, were fixed on the arms of both wheels, and several excursions up and down the river, made with them. Their dip was 7 inches, or rather more, for their upper edges were half an inch below the surface. They were next removed from one wheel, and left on the other, as the standard by which to compare the effects of different shaped ones. They were distinguished as No. 1. Nearly all the rest were formed from them: *i. e.* by removing portions from one part, and adding them to others, as will be seen in the following diagrams. In this way there was no danger of making, through mistake, one set of blades of larger or of less superficial surface than others, since no calculation of their areas was required.

In all the figures, the paddles are supposed to sweep through the water in the position as represented, the lowest sides being those which descend lowest in the fluid.

Fig. 41 is formed by cutting off the lower angles of fig.

40, and transferring the pieces to the upper ones, making a right-angled triangle, with sides 10 inches, and hypothenuse 14. (By mistake the upper corners were cut away, so as to leave the area of these blades 48 square inches instead of 49.) Eight of these were fixed on the wheel (see B, fig. 39), to compete with the same number of fig. 40, on A, both having seven and a half inches dip.

It will be obvious that, as both sets were attached to the same shaft, if one proved more efficient than the other, the boat would be turned from a straight course, and be inclined, more or less abruptly, to the weaker, or less efficient set. The result was, that those marked fig. 40 overcame fig. 41, and though only in a small degree, yet quite sufficient to establish their superior effect on the vessel's progress.—As we were not always out of the influence of tides and slight breezes, each experiment embraced excursions in various directions on the river. Once or twice the boat went straight as an arrow, but eventually the square paddles got the better of the triangular ones. These dipped into the water with little noise, and threw it off behind from their points.

Most of the experiments were made in smooth water, and, except slight currents—aqueous and aerial—under the most favorable circumstances. Two persons occupied the boat, and the greatest care was exercised in preserving the shaft in a horizontal position. When results were doubtful, the experiments were repeated, and, generally, several times.

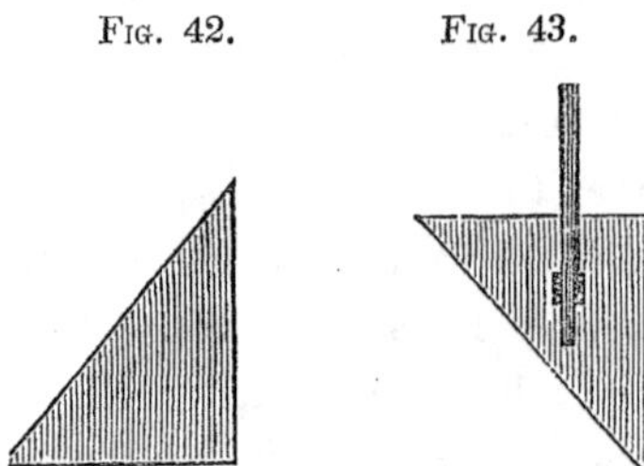

The same paddles, fig. 41, were next attached to the arms in the position represented in the margin, and distinguished as fig. 43, the upper side being, as in all other instances, 13 inches from the centre of the axis. Through repeated trials, they overcame the test paddles, fig. 40, and in a rather more marked manner than fig. 40 surpassed fig. 41. They entered the water silently, but observers on shore thought they raised more water behind, but did not raise it as high as fig. 40.—Their points were nearly three inches lower in the water than the lower edges of fig. 40. The boat described a circle of 400 feet, and another of 600.

The same blades were next tried as fig. 42. From the experiment fig. 43, it was inferable that, if inverted, the effect of the blade on the boat would have a longer sweep through the water. Such was the fact, and to such a degree, that first two, and then four, were removed from the arms, when the remaining four were found equal to the eight of fig. 40.

Fig. 44. Fig. 45.

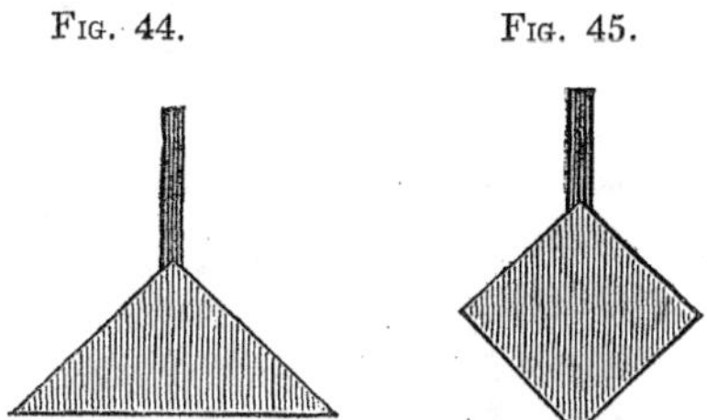

Lastly, the same blades were turned into the position of fig. 44 (being fig. 41 reversed).—The boat was turned on 40 under all circumstances, describing circles from 80 to 150 feet in diameter. Four of them equalled eight of No. 40. They were thought to throw off more water behind than their competitors, which, from the greater extent of their extremities, was probably true.

The next form tried was fig. 40, placed in the position of fig. 45. These turned the boat round againt the test ones, in circles varying from 50 to 200 feet. We then tried six of them against the other eight, when there was little observable difference in the result. Four were found superior, but three were unequal to them. These, of course, entered the water without jarring, and threw it off at their points.

Fig. 46, formed by removing the upper corners below, as in the figure, seemed to have the advantage of fig. 45. Four were superior to eight of fig. 40. It was supposed that a slight accession of resistance to the lower ends,

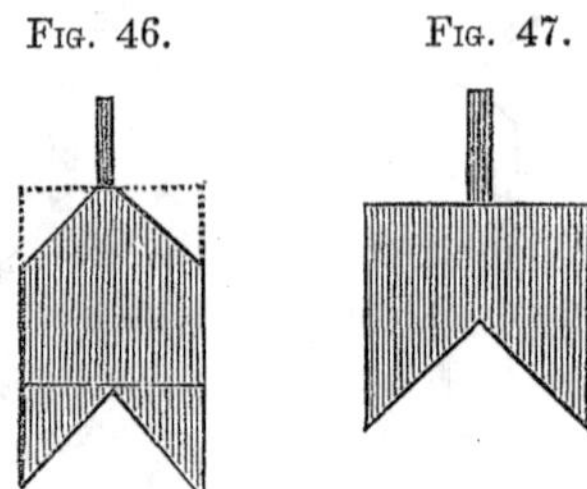
Fig. 46. Fig. 47.

sweeping through the water, might be derived from opposing currents meeting in the forks, but we had no means to ascertain if it existed.

Figure 47 is cut out of plates eight inches square, with one-fourth (minus a superficial inch) removed, as shown in the figure. After several excursions, these were thought to exhibit a very slight advantage over fig. 40; but from subsequent tests, they seemed to be balanced. Fig. 48 had a decided preponderance over their competitors. Six predominated slightly over the latter, and four seemed nearly equal to them.

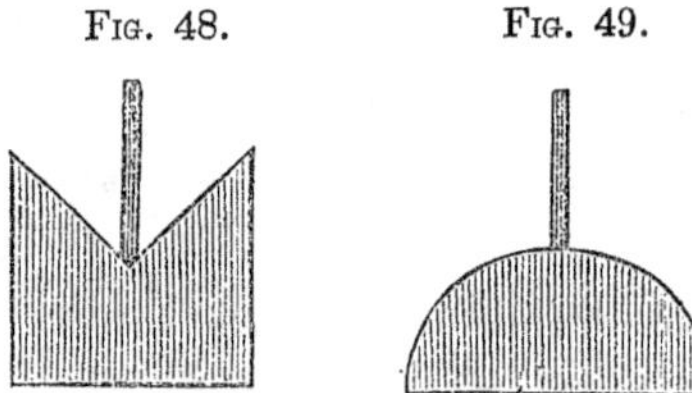
Fig. 48. Fig. 49.

Fig. 49 was a semicircle. They turned the boat in circles varying (from light winds and tides) from 30 to 150 feet. Four were thought equal, and sometimes superior, to eight of fig. 40. It is demonstrable that these blades are less effective, though in a very small degree, than those marked fig. 44, and, when reversed, more powerful than fig. 41.

Fig. 50 was formed as represented but not tried, as it was evident their value would be nearly that of fig. 44, probably a shade above them, but too minute to be detected, except in perfectly still water.

Fig. 51 is a right-angled triangle, 7 inches across the top, and ending in a point nearly 14 inches below it. These were more effective than those of fig. 40. They entered the water without jarring.

The same were attached to the arms in the position of fig. 52, and were unable to compete with fig. 40. The latter had a slight advantage over them.

Fig. 50. Fig. 51.

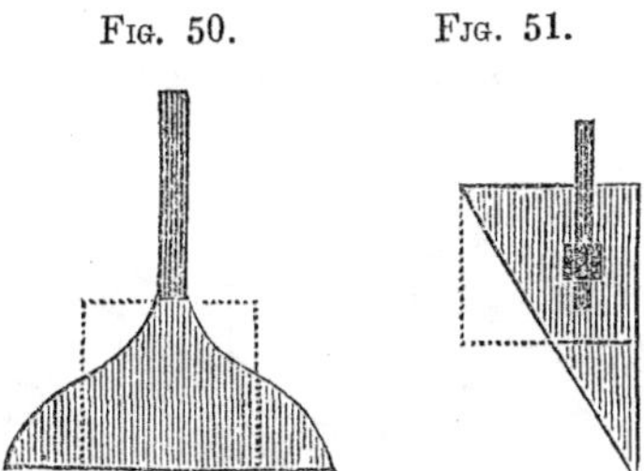

They were next reversed, as fig. 53, when they proved effective as fig. 44, and 49—four being equally so as the eight opposed to them.

They were finally changed to fig. 54, when the boat was turned so rapidly, as to make it difficult, with a wide oar, to keep her in one direction. Four were removed, and then she described a circle in less than 50 feet. Two more taken away, leaving only a couple to act against the eight on the other wheel, and to which they proved equal.

From these experiments, it appears that, with equal areas, and equal dip, triangular blades may be rendered twice as effective as ordinary rectangular ones. This is made manifest by figs. 44, 49, and 53,—four of the former equalling eight of the latter. And this, too, while the propelling surface of the smaller number was half that of the greater; for the four were as long in making a revolution, as were the eight. Hence, the speed of a boat may be increased by diminishing the number of her paddles—a fact still further elucidated by fig. 54.

Fig. 52. Fig. 53. Fig. 54.

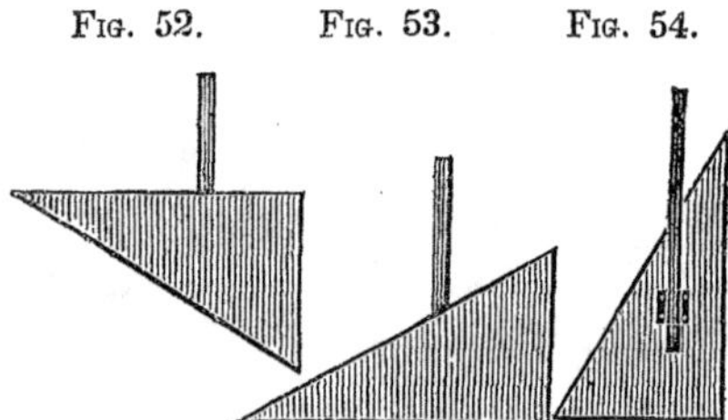

There can, says Mr. Ewbank, be little doubt, that the greater the velocity of a steamer's wheels, the fewer (within certain limits) should be the blades; and that, at the rate at which some of our boats go, the number might be reduced with advantage. Some have three, others four, and in more than one vessel, without any load on board, submerged at each wheel. In these cases, is it not evident that each blade, on entering, plunges, not, as it ought, in water undisturbed, but into that which preceding ones have already broken up and set in motion towards the stern? It would seem that one in the act of plunging, another sweeping under the shaft, and a third leaving the surface, are all that are necessary to be kept up; and that a greater number, as regards the speed of a boat, is positively injurious. Yet under a vague idea of attaining a higher speed, the number of paddles has frequently been nearly doubled.

Snow, as every person knows, causes the wheels of land locomotives to slip upon, instead of rolling over the rail. They revolve as usual, but the carriages make little progress, hence much of the power spent on them is expended to no purpose. So it is with paddle-wheels: a boat never progresses in the ratio of their revolutions, because of the yielding medium in which, and against which, they act. They slip always—a result, to some extent, inevitable when massive solids wade through fluids. The distance between the Atlantic steamers' docks, in Liverpool and New-York, has been calculated at 3023 miles, but their paddles, in each trip, pass over a space varying from 5000 to 8000 miles. In

Fig. 55.

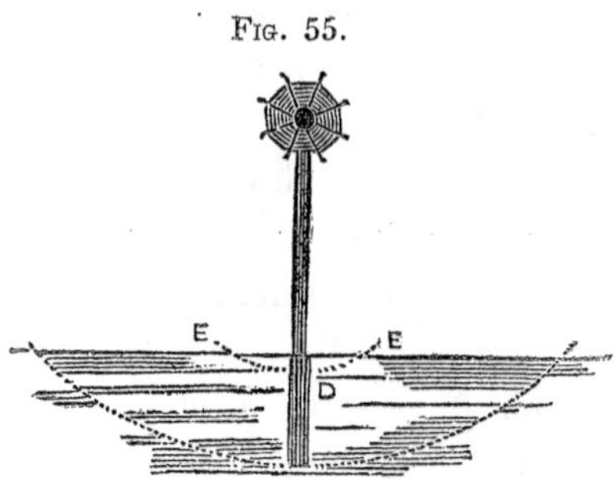

steamers unaided by sails, the disproportion is often greater. Now can this be modified, by giving the paddles a better hold on the fluid they sweep through? The experiments with blades 42, 43, 44, 45, 46, 47, 48, 49, 51, 53, and 54, furnish replies to the interrogatory.

The moral of the foregoing experiments is this:—As the propelling power of a paddle is greatest at its lower or outer extremity, and diminishes to nothing at the surface, so its face should enlarge with the dip, and be nothing, or next to nothing, above. Let D, fig. 55, represent the end of an ordinary blade, or paddle. Its upper part barely touches the water, and only for the moment it is in the position shown. But suppose it were immersed to the line E E,—say four or five inches—it would even then be no sooner under, than above the surface again, so brief would be its immersion. The lower edge, in the meanwhile, would sweep along the extended curve there delineated.

Fig. 56.

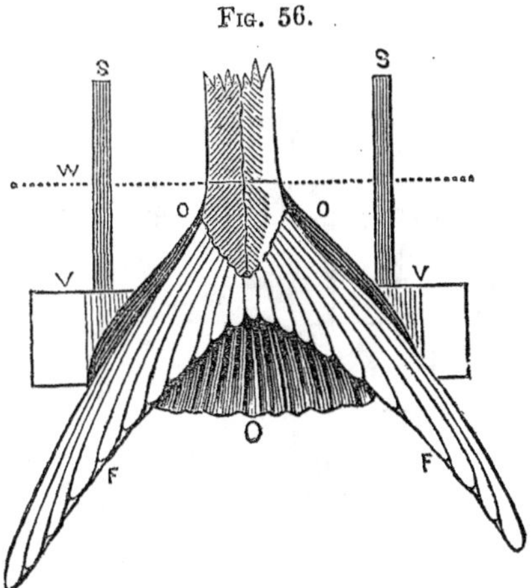

The Report again says "the extension of the lower part of the paddle and its contraction above, is nature's own plan," and this it sets forth by the annexed diagrams of the tails of fast and slow fishes. Fig. 56 shows the combination of the tails of a fast and slow swimming fish and a steamer's blade. The dark part of the figure O O O is the caudal paddle of a fress-water bass, a slow swimmer, and to give it the speed of the dolphin it should be constructed with the lobes, F F (dolphin) which will have the same material as O O O, but the propelling lever will extend further from the fulcrum, and will have a longer sweep, and therefore exert their force to propel for a longer period on the water.

Fig. 57.

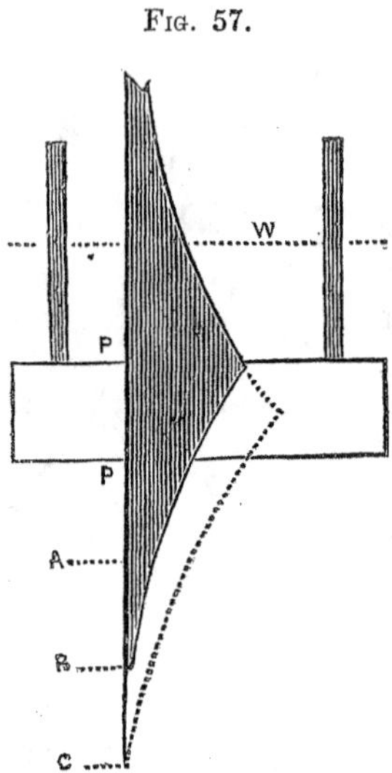

Suppose W, the water line and the parallelogram V V, a steamer's blade, attached to the arms S S. The vessel's speed is required to be increased. How is it to be attained? Almost always by adding to the surface laterally at V V. Thus, as has been remarked, the ocean steamers now in progress in New York—supposed to embrace every possible improvement—have the paddle planks 14 feet, (some boats have them 22 feet!) stretching that distance from each side of the vessels; as if half the surface, disposed after nature's mode, would not be equally sufficient and with the same power; for, saving of power is as essential a result of improvement in form, as of approaching the truth in any other particular.

Suppose P P, fig. 57, represents one of those enormous blades about to be enlarged to make a vessel go faster, is it not apparent that by altering its figure to that shown by the dark tint, the rule of nature being followed, superior results must ensue? and this not by adding to, but actually dispensing with about one half of the propelling surface. Were the boundaries extended to the dotted lines, the area would still be nearly one third less than the original. In this type of blade a quality unknown in common ones is relieved, viz., every horizontal section bears a like amount of strain, and contributes equally to the work done, although their areas differ so materially; thus the portion included between the lines A P, from the larger sweep it has to take, equals the larger portion between P P; and for the same reason, the section A B, equals A P;—increased range compensating for diminished surface. [This is a point which, I believe, no engineer has yet brought out. The idea is a new one in artificial propelling.] In this, also, we see there is nothing accidental, or without deep meaning, in nature's works.

The ordinary mode of increasing the efficacy of paddles has been to widen the levers instead of lengthening them. Thus the jar arising from 14 to 20 feet planks striking the water, is a constant source of destruction to both vessel and machinery, while with blades, as figured above, it is annihilated, and the enormous amount of power consumed by it, saved.

Having presented the main points of the Report of Mr.

Ewbank, Commissioner of Patents, so as to convey a clear idea of his experiments and the conclusion at which he arrived, as to what constituted the best form of blades for propelling vessels, we will now conclude our extracts from the same with the following illustration:—

Fig. 58.

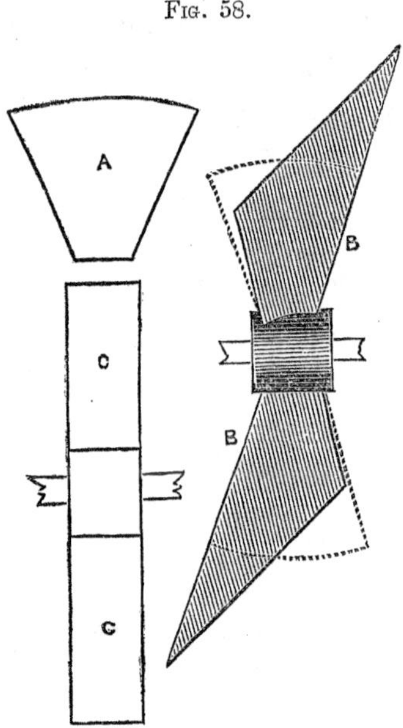

Devices for readily lengthening and shortening the arms, so as to vary the dip with the changing draught of a vessel, and accurately to adapt it to the power of her engines, are worth adopting.

The principle is of course equally applicable to stern submerged propellers, revolving sculls or screws. In these the ancient forms are the latest also. Those last patented were proposed over a century ago. A is an outline of Woodcroft's, patented here in 1846, and in England previously. Those of Stevens, Loper, Ericson, Smith, and a host of others, have the same sectorial form. Their resemblance to the tails of slow-swimming fish is obvious to every eye. Would it not be better to make each more like the lobe of the most agile and swift, as at B B? A rectangular blade—not unlike one belonging to a paddle-wheel attached to the axis endwise, as at C C, has also been recommended, though on what grounds it is not easy to perceive. The Great Britain steamship had blades resembling those figured at C C.

Mr. Ewbank inculcates the lesson of following *nature* in mechanical philosophy, as being the best guide; and in reference to propulsion, he says, "if ever nature took extra pains to teach engineers a lesson, she has done it here, and let them never forget that nature and natural philosophy are *never* at variance." While we subscribe to the latter sentiment, we would state that the only difficulty in the way of following after nature, lies in our acquaintance with, or ignorance of, *nature's laws*,—and more than this, man must look to more than the sight of his eyes to follow after in nature, so as to guide him in mechanical philosophy. The God of Heaven has given him reason to lead him above a mere copyist—to be a *creator* in his own world, himself—because he is formed in the image of his Creator, who made him *lord* of the world.

If man had never soared above natural presented objects, he never would have constructed a carriage to move on wheels. The first locomotive was constructed with legs, like a deer, because the swiftest of animals used such propellers, but such a method of propulsion was not equal to rolling wheels; and in what part of nature's labyrinth did Stephenson get his first lesson of the "Rocket?" The same kind of reasoning is applicable to the paddle-wheels of steamboats. No fish or fowl uses rotary propellers; all of them employ reciprocating propellers; and it was copying after nature which led the ingenious Earl of Stanhope to employ what is termed the "Duck's-foot propeller." It is well known, as we have shown in the preceding parts of our history of propellers, that the devices for this purpose are "legion," while none have been able to maintain the field against the oblong rectangular blades of the paddle-wheels, as they are at present constructed. We must consider every obstacle which has to be overcome; and when we reflect upon the mighty storms of the Atlantic, the huge waves beating against the vessel's sides like battering rams, we must look to strength in construction, as well as to the best form for speed. The race-horse for the race-course, the hunter for the wood and the wild.

We believe, however, that our screw propellers should adopt the ideas presented in Fig. 58; the improvement appears to be like a self-evident axiom, requiring no debate.

BIRAM'S PADDLE WHEEL.

FIG. 59.

It has often been attempted to place the floats of paddle-wheels oblique, in order to allow the blades to enter the water with an increasing surface, upon the principle of the wedge, to reduce the tremulous motion of the vessel, caused by the direct action of the common blades upon the water. Among the many plans for this purpose, we present one patented by a Mr. Biram, an English engineer.

In figure 59 we have a side view, and figure 60 is a perspective view.

In this the floats, A, are supposed to be made of iron plate, and consist of two parts; one part is a flat plate, riveted to the ring and arm, and this is met by a second plate, slightly curved and set obliquely to the axis of the paddle. By this arrangement the float enters the water gradually, and communicates to it an angular motion at right angles to its own plane. The water, as it recedes from the oblique float, is thrown upon the parallel side-plate, and being thus confined, it is supposed to give the same amount of reaction as would be produced by action of the common float.

Fig. 60.

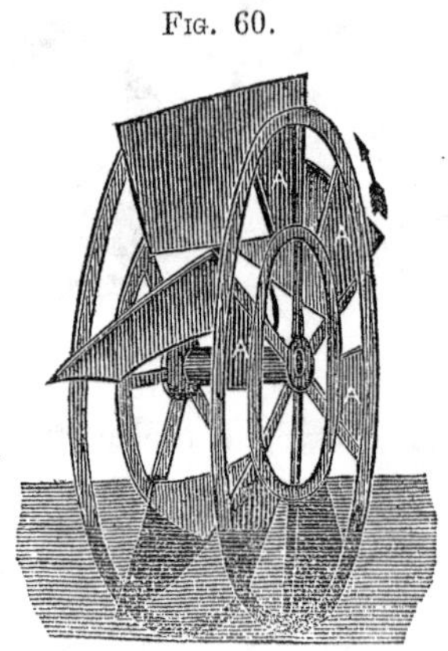

It will be observed that the action of the floats upon the water is angular, as is fully shown.

The placing of a single paddle obliquely on the face of the wheel, is something which has not been thought of by a single individual, but by quite a number. The paddle wheel here presented (Fig. 61) was fairly tried on a very fine steamboat, called the Superb, built in Glasgow, Scotland, a place famous for steamship-building, and for experi-

DOUBLE OBLIQUE PADDLES.

Fig. 61.

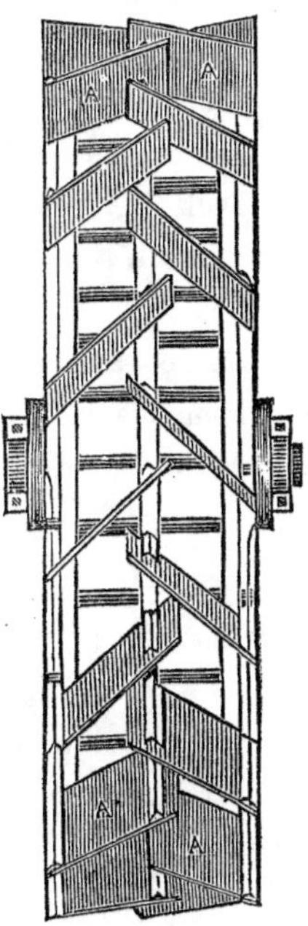

ments in marine navigation, and was thought for a while to be superior to the common paddle-wheel, but on the whole, after a fair trial of its merits, the old wheel towered above it in utility, and laid it on the shelf.

Instead of the floats A A A in this paddle-wheel, being placed parallel to the shaft, they are fixed at a considerable angle to it, and in alternate opposition to one another, each float projecting beyond that opposite to it. By placing the floats in these relative positions, the amount of direct resistance upon the water does not seem to be diminished; while the oblique direction in which the floats enter into and emerge from the water, as well as the water being drawn as it were into the interior of the wheel between the floats, there is less of that back lift and dashing of the water against the sides of the vessel, than there is with the common paddles.

The principal advantage—and we consider it a very important desideratum which this paddle seems to possess—is the diminution of tremor in the vessel.

RENNIE'S EXPERIMENTS IN PADDLE WHEELS.

The Civil Engineer and Architect's Journal, of September, 1849, contains an article from George Rennie, so well known as an experienced engineer, on the subject of the form of paddles, which has been represented in the Franklin Journal. It refers to the experiments of Mr. Ewbank with marked respect, and says :—

The facts developed by his experiments may be briefly stated: they are as follows :—

1st. That, with equal areas and equal dip, triangular blades may be rendered twice as effective as ordinary rectangular ones; and this, too, while the propelling surface of the smaller number of floats was only half that of the greater.

2d. That, as the propelling power of a paddle is greatest at its greater or outer extremity, and diminishes to nothing at the surface, so its face should enlarge with the dip, and be nothing above—in imitation of the tails of fishes, the wings of birds, &c.

3d. That the fewer the number of paddles on a wheel the better, provided one be always kept in full play; and,

4th. That it would be more advantageous to point or fork them as proposed, to evade the jar of their striking the surface.

Fig. 62.

(Modifications of Ordinary System.)

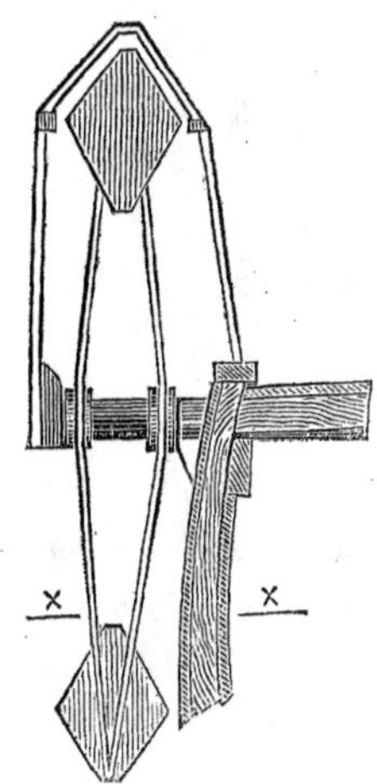

In the year 1831, he says, my attention was attracted to this subject during the investigations undertaken for the purpose of ascertaining the laws of the friction and resistance of solids in motion in fluids, such as air and water; when, on causing discs or plates of metal to rotate round a fixed axle, by means of weights descending through given spaces and times, it was found that when a certain portion (one-fourth) of a rectangular disc or fan was intercepted,

Fig. 63.

(Improved Trapezium System.)

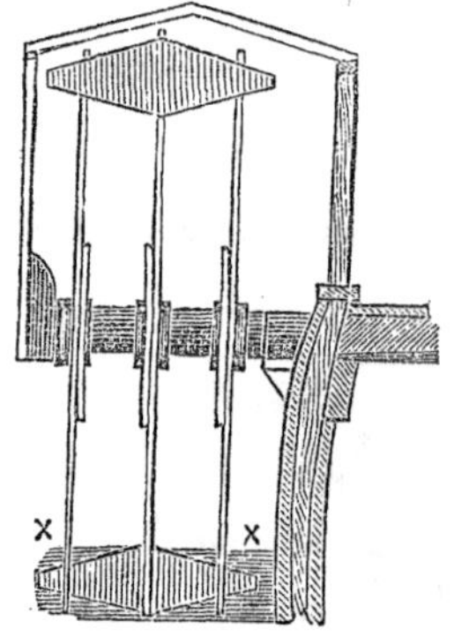

from the interior part of the rectangle, so as to approximate to the form of a duck's foot, the resistance, whether through air or water, was the same—or, in other words, the resistance with three triangular or duck-footed floats was as great as previously with four rectangular floats. This apparent paradox was, however, accounted for on the principle of the interior or detrimental portion of the rectangular float being removed.

IMPROVED TRIANGULAR SYSTEM, WHEN THE VESSEL IS UPRIGHT.

FIG. 64.

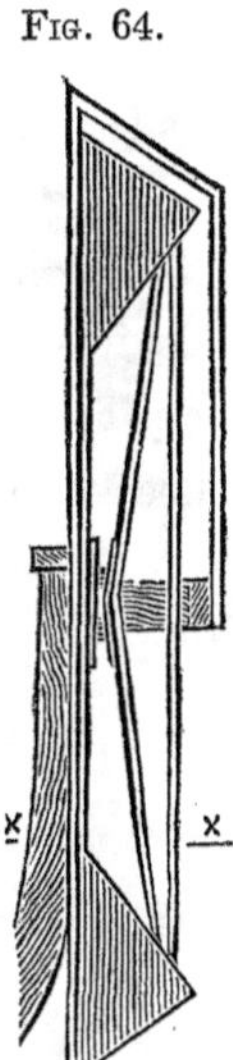

A series of experiments on two other vessels was again made in the years 1839, 1840, and 1841, by applying different shaped floats to paddle wheels of different diameters and widths, and on steam vessels of different powers, of from 6 to 90 horses—an abstract of some of which was published in 1840.

The following are the particulars of the "African," when tried in 1837, previous to her being tried in 1841 :

Length between perpendiculars,	109 feet,	11 inches.	
Extreme breadth, - -	24 "	10 "	
Mean draught, - - -	9 "	$4\frac{1}{2}$ "	
Depth, - - - -	10 "	0 "	

Nominal power of engines (by Maudsleys and Field) 45 horses, or 90 horses together.

Number of strokes made by the engine per minute, 20 to 30.

Barometer gauge, 24 to $26\frac{3}{4}$ inches.

Area of immersal midship section, 150 square feet.

Mean diameter of the paddle-wheels, 14·7.

Area of the immersal rectangular floats, on the cycloidal or Galloway system, twelve in number, 7 feet in length and 1 foot 9 inches in breadth; thus presenting an area of from 57 to 60 square feet, being a ratio of 1 foot of float to 1·6 midship section.

IMPROVED TRIANGULAR SYSTEM WHEN THE VESSEL IS INCLINED.

Fig. 65.

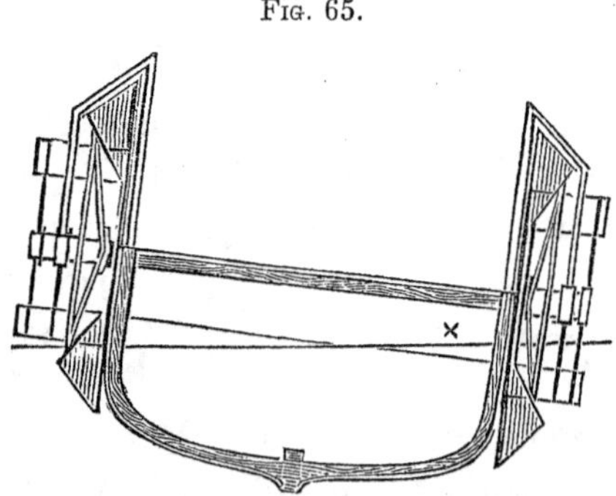

When this trial was made, in 1837, at the measured mile in Long Reach, her average speed, of six trials each, was 9·174 statute miles per hour, with her rectangular floats. Subsequently she was employed for towing, and other purposes, and had never undergone any other repairs than in her engines, and had never been in dry dock; her bottom was consequently foul, and covered with green weeds when tried with the trapezium floats in 1841.

Experiments on H. M. steamer "African," with trapezium floats.—All the rectangular floats, twelve in number on each wheel, were removed, and twelve trapezium floats were fixed to the interior and middle rings of each wheel. X X is the water-line.

Thus making the area of the immersed floats 34 square feet.

Number of revolutions made by engines, 23½ per minute.

Mean speed of vessel in statute miles, 9·1.

Mean diameter of wheels, 17 feet.

Comparing the whole of the experiments, when tried in still water, under the most favorable circumstances, and when tried in the "African," under the unfavorable circumstances of foul bottom, and difference of the powers of the engines, the conclusion is in favor of the trapezium floats. The truth of the principle is confirmed by Mr. Ewbank, and by the laws which govern the forms of the tails of fishes, the feet of aquatic birds, and the wings of birds and insects, whereby the means are so admirably suited to the ends; and the triangular form, proposed by Mr. Ewbank for paddle floats, entirely confirms the view I took of the subject in the years 1839 and 1840.

HOLLOW CONICAL PADDLES.

FIG. 66.

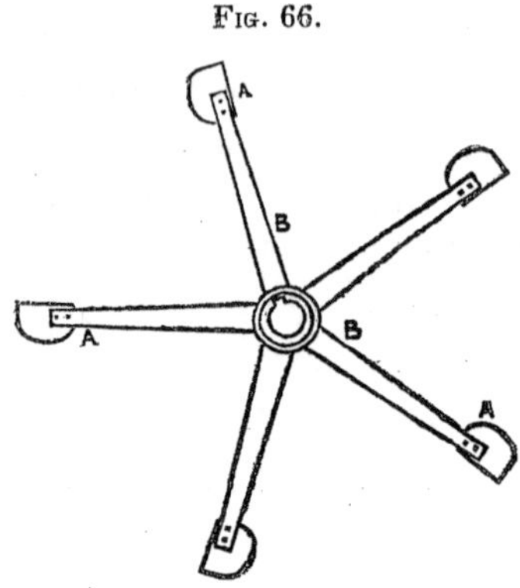

The accompanying engraving represents the paddles made of hollow cones, A A, made of metal of a sufficient thickness, and cut at the vertex at right angles to the plane of its base, so as to divide them into two equal parts, which are affixed to the arms, B B, as represented. These half-cones may vary in number. The best form is the half-cone with the angle of 32 degrees at the plane of the base; but by extending the surface of the half-cone a greater propelling force is the result. This invention is the subject of a patent in England; the inventor being a Gent., as he styles himself, named Thomas Parlour, of Holloway.

STEVENS' NEW PLAN TO INCREASE THE SPEED OF STEAMBOATS.

FIG. 67.

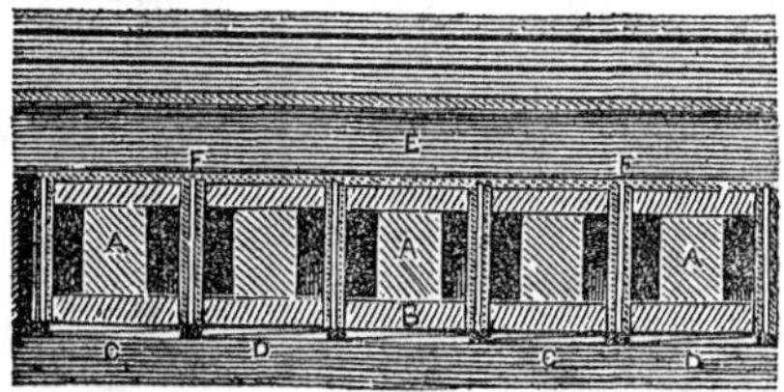

A great number have heard that Mr. Francis B. Stevens, of Hoboken, N. Y., had invented a new plan for increasing the speed of steamboats, by interposing a stratum of air between the immersed surface of the vessel and the water, but few know any more about it, although it has been patented both in America and in Europe, since 1847.

Fig. 67 is a longitudinal section through the bottom of the vessel; and fig. 68 is a transverse section; A A are the timbers of the bottom of the vessel, and B is

FIG. 68.

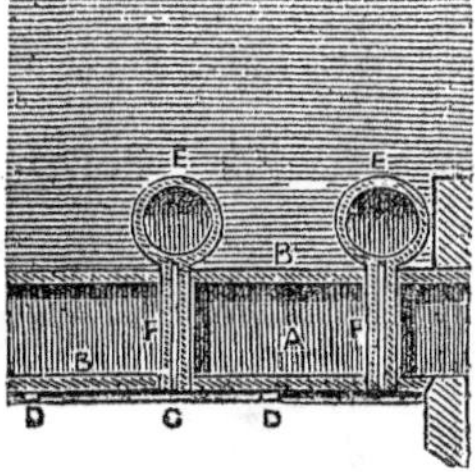

the planking; C C are pieces of planking of an angular shape, shown first on the planking forming a series of recesses upon the bottom of the vessel, or these recesses may be formed out of the planking itself. These recesses are in a series, divided by strips, D, and run along the whole length of the vessel. Running fore and aft along the whole bottom, inside, are trunks, E E, from which are small branch pipes, F F, through the bottom of the vessel, one at least for each recess, and terminating on the outside, behind the angular shaped pieces, C C. This position of the pipes behind the base of the angles, C C, prevents the water from entering the pipes when the vessel is in motion. The bases of the angular pieces being laid towards the stern of the vessel, the main pipes, E, communicate with the air-compressing apparatus, by which the air is forced in through the system of conduits, and the recesses kept charged with a stratum of atmospheric air.

A steamboat constructed upon this plan has been employed by Mr. Stevens, and was laid up a short time since at Hoboken, affording an opportunity for examining her construction. It does not appear to embrace any economical principle, whereby, with the same power, the speed of a steamboat can be increased in the least.

CHAPTER VII.

SCREW PROPELLERS.

It is not possible for us to assign the invention of the screw propeller to the first inventor, whoever he may be. The screw has been claimed by America and England. Mr. Hutchings, in his defence of John Fitch, exhibits his steamboat with side-wheels, and a screw at the stern likewise.

The accompanying figure, 69, was the plan of a propeller proposed by Woodcroft, having one spiral on each

Fig. 69.

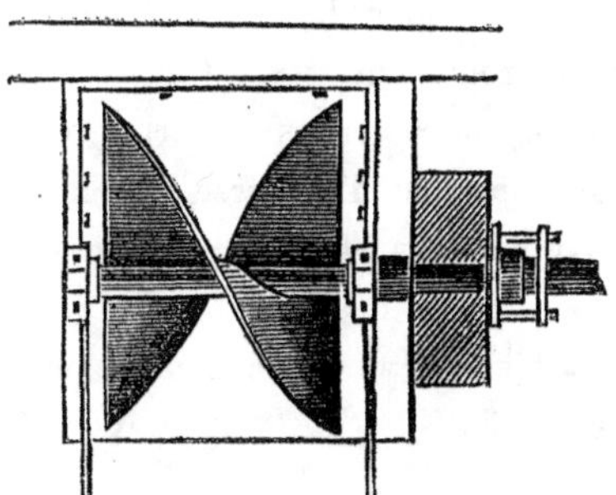

side. The form of the screw was that of an increasing pitch—the correct form. An account of it was first published by Partingdon, in 1834. It was a screw wrapped round a shaft, and the increasing pitch of the blade enabled each part to act upon the water. The principle of this invention consists in making the water a nut and the spiral a screw, acting upon the water, to propel the vesssel.

It was not until 1839 that the principle of propelling steamships by a screw-blade was fairly brought before the world, and for this we are indebted, as almost every adult will remember, to Mr. F. P. Smith, of London. He was the man who first made the screw propeller practically useful. Aided by spirited capitalists, he built a large steamer named the "Archimedes," and the results obtained from her at once arrested public attention. This engraving represents the double-threaded screw employed on the Archimedes. A large proportion of the complete screw having no useful effect, a great portion of the central part of this one was cut away, so that the form should offer but little resistance to the water, yet act upon it by the blades so as to obtain full power in propulsion. But this screw had not a very good effect upon the water, as the arms formed by the ends of the blades obstructed its free passage. Although the trial of the Archimedes was very satisfactory, it was evident that there was a great deal of what is termed *slip*, by such a screw, and this fact was always made manifest when the vessel was backed.

FOUR-BLADED FRENCH PROPELLER.

Fig. 70.

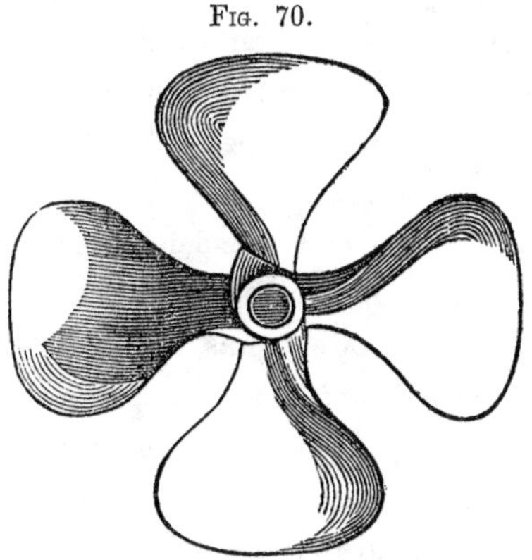

This is a propeller which was employed on a French Mail Boat, named the Napoleon, in 1842. Fig. 70 exhibits a front, and fig. 71 a side view. This propeller was fixed in a space or opening abaft the usual stern-post (to which, in an ordinary vessel, the rudder would be hung), and inside of another stern-post, which was erected on a prolongation of the keel, farther aft, for sustaining the rudder, so as to leave a space between the two posts, for the reception of the propeller. The centre of the propeller was 6 feet beneath the surface of the water; its diameter was 7 feet 6 inches, and the highest point of its periphery was 2 feet 3 inches below the water line, when the mean draft of water aft was about 11·82 feet.

Four propellers of the same diameter, but of different forms, were made, of cast-iron, and were tried with various success. The propellers had been altered several times; and it was found that within certain limits, by cutting away the ends so as to shorten the length of the screw, which had also the effect of diminishing the surface of the blades, the speed of the vessel was increased, and the vibration was reduced; a portion of this effect had, however, been attributed to using four arms. A propeller with three blades, occupying the whole of the circle, was first tried; others which presented less central surface answered better; and the best (which is still in use) had four blades, which occupied six-tenths of the area of the circle, when viewed in the direction of the axis, leaving four-tenths of that area vacant for the free escape of the water between the blades, whose obliquity was such as to produce an advance of 10 feet 3 inches in a revolution.

Fig. 71.

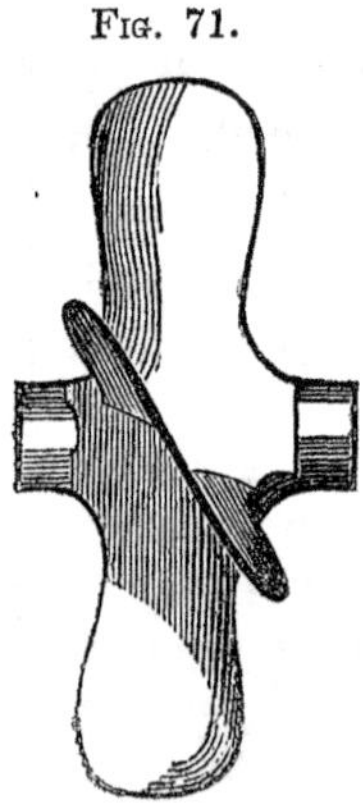

The motion was communicated to the propeller by a spur-wheel of 126 teeth, working into a pinion of 20 teeth, which gave nearly $6\frac{1}{3}$ revolutions for each stroke of the engine, or about 120 revolutions of the propeller per minute. The ordinary speed of the vessel, without any sails being used, was 10 knots, or $11\frac{1}{2}$ statute miles per hour.

CONOIDAL SCREW PROPELLER.

This is a screw, fig. 72, of three blades, invented by Messrs. Rennie, of London, and applied by them, in 1839, to a steamer named the Dwarf. Friction wheels were first used for giving motion to the propeller, but on account of their noise and slipping, they were abandoned, and spur-wheels, with wooden teeth, substituted. It made about 150 revolutions per minute. The advantage of this form of screw over the one represented last, is an increasing pitch, so formed that while the propeller is rotating on its axis, the vessel is advancing—thus making far less slip. These blades are curved conoids, therefore they have variable curves approximating to angles from 27° to 30°. It was 5 feet 10 inches diameter, and had an area of about 15 square feet, and in smooth water propelled the vessel at the rate of 12 miles per hour,—the vessel being 164 tons burden, with engines of 70 horse power. In 1843 this vessel ran 200 miles in 23 hours, and used 10 tons of coal in 27 hours, from the time of getting up the steam. This propeller had a slip of one-eighth. The superiority of the conoid propeller was set forth to be the best, as being formed after nature's laws and the swiftest of fishes. The opening towards the centre of motion by reducing the arms of the screw blades, as far as strength would allow (as the rotative motion towards the centre is less than the circumference), reduced a tendency to centrifugal action on the water. The gradual alteration of the angle of the blade to the axis of the screw or outward path of the vessel, affords a greater onward action of the blade at the entrance, whilst it gradually curves round to nearly a right angle with the path, so as to leave the water without causing a revulsion. The salmon, when it makes a run, puts down all its side fins, and solely by the oblique action of the tail, is propelled forward with great force and speed, so as to leave the water without revulsion; the flexible nature and curving form of the tail contributes to this object.

Fig. 72.

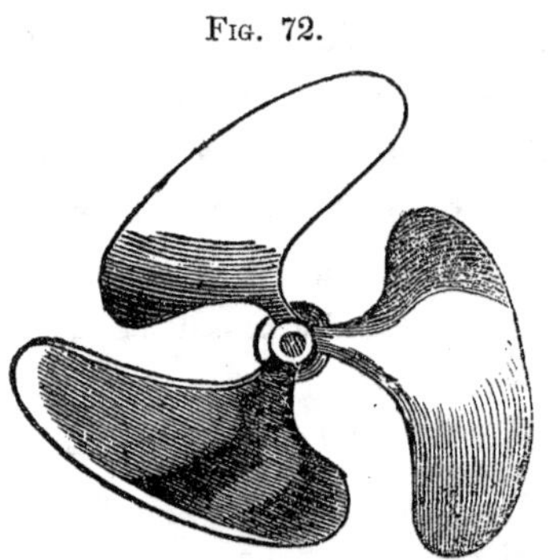

THE LIVERPOOL SCREW.

Figures 73 and 74 represent what is termed the "Liverpool Screw." It is made on Woodcroft's plan. It has four blades, with broad shovel ends, set at a mean angle of 45°. It is termed the *Liverpool* screw, because it was applied to the steamer of that name.

Fig. 73.

With respect to a screw of equal, and one of an increasing pitch, Mr. Woodcroft tried a fair experiment with two such, of equal area, placed at the stern of a vessel, and he found that the screw of an increasing pitch gave the greatest impulse to the vessel, turning it from its direct course—thus showing that the two forces were unequal—the greatest effect being produced by the screw of an increasing pitch.

FIG. 74.

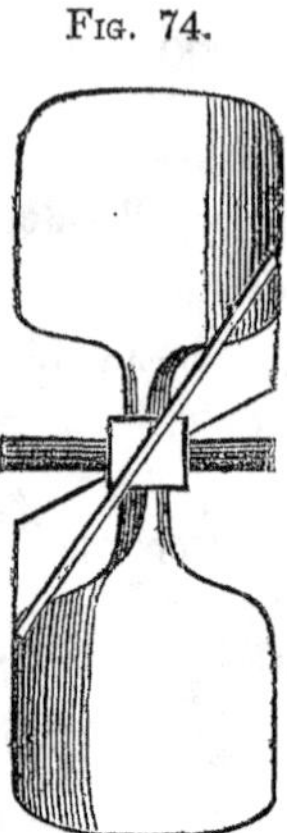

The amount of slip in a screw is not so well known, owing to the difference of opinion about the best form and the proper diameter of the screws. The four-bladed Liverpool Screw, was enlarged three times, and every time improved the speed of the vessel. The speed of the engines remaining the same. This was no doubt owing to its being too small at first. The area of a propeller must be in proportion to the body to be moved, but what that area should be precisely, is not yet generally understood. In paddles it is well known that the vessel does not move through the same space as the wheels, the difference being 1000 for paddles, and 739 for the speed of the vessel.

The following formula from Tredgold is laid down by Galloway to determine what pitch a screw should have:— "To the speed in feet per minute add the amount of slip, and divide by the number of revolutions, the resultand is the answer. Thus, intended speed of vessel 10 miles per hour or (860) feet per minute; the amount of slip 2 miles or (172) feet per minute; number of revolutions, 120 feet per minute:—

$$\frac{860+172}{120}=8{\cdot}6 \text{ feet.}$$

ERICSON PROPELLER.

Fig. 75.

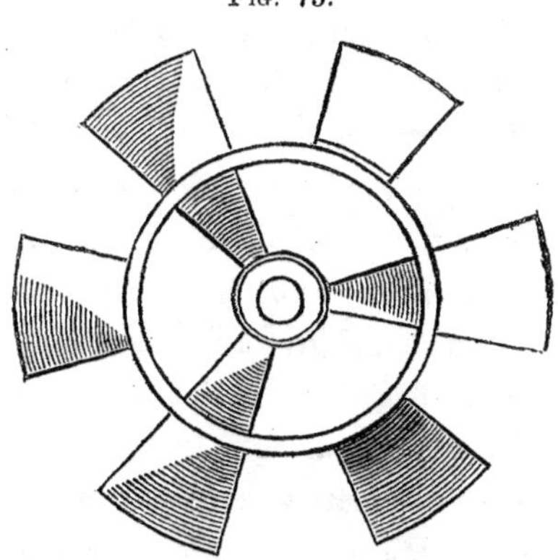

It is a number of years since the screw propeller was introduced into America, and in March 1834, a patent was granted to John B. Emerson for a submerged propeller. The first specification of Emerson was a bungling business, and the patent with it was not worth a snuff, as it had not a correct drawing attached; but a second drawing was filed after the patent was granted, and in a trial for infringement of his patent against Hogg & Delameter, the jury found a verdict for Emerson, and against the propeller known as "Ericson's Propeller," which is now presented as applied to the Princeton, an American frigate. The Princeton was 164 feet long, with a breadth of beam of 30 feet; the depth of the hold was 22 feet 6 inches, the draught of water was 17 feet 6 inches, and the burthen about 700 tons; the propeller was 14 feet in diameter, with six blades, and made from 33 to 36 revolutions per minute, at which rate the vessel's speed was stated to be nearly 14 miles per hour. The engines were about 400 horse power; they were of peculiar construction, having two steam cylinders, or chests, containing vibrating pistons or flaps, with cranks upon the ends of the suspending pivots, both these were coupled by connecting rods to a main crank on the driving shaft; the length of these cranks being so proportioned that their alternate vibrations should give a rotary motion to the main crank, and thus act directly upon the propeller, without the intervention of bands or gearing.

We have seen many flattering notices of connecting the pistons by direct action with the propeller shaft, and have heard many objections to the use of cog gearing in propellers, but the argument seems all to be in favor of the cog gearing, when the master wheel has good wooden teeth. The "City of Glasgow" is connected in this way, and if there is one fact stronger than another to give force to her arrangement of gearing, it is her success.

FIG. 76.

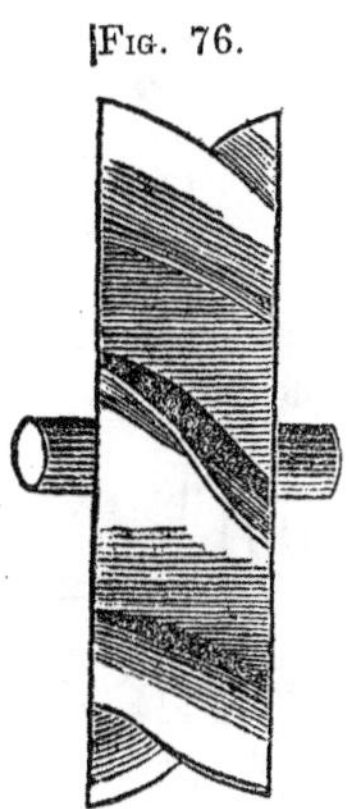

The accompanying engravings, 75 and 76, represent the Ericsŏn propeller applied to the Princeton and to the Robert Stockton, the latter vessel being tried successfully on the river Thames as a tug boat, in 1839. It was named after Commodore Stockton, who introduced the screw into the American navy. The propeller, figures 73 and 74, some have contended was the best form of all, as the broad shovel ends were fixed at a mean angle of 45°. It was the one preferred by Woodcroft, as adopted, and termed the "Liverpool Screw."

The advantage of the Ericson screw, is in having a ring within the arms, whereby any number of blades can be fixed, and a large area of surface obtained.

LOPER'S PROPELLER.

FIG. 77.

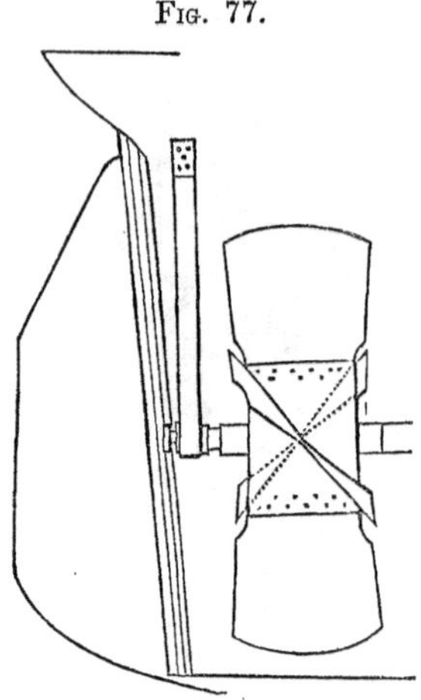

This propeller is the invention of Captain Loper, of Philadelphia, and its good character is so well established, that it requires no further eulogy than to say, that more of these kind of propellers are now employed on vessels in the United States than any other, and on vessels of every class of burden, from the small canal boat to the first-class steamship.

The accompanying engraving represents the Loper Propeller, as applied to the trial U. S. Revenue Steamer "Spencer." The diameter of the propeller is eight feet, width of blade at hub two feet three inches—at outside four feet four inches. The angle of the blades at the hub 30°, at the outside 54°. It was driven by the common intermediate gearing of cog-wheel and pinion.

Screw propulsion has received the earnest attention of eminent engineers in America and Europe, and is now regarded as more economical than side wheels, but only as auxiliary to sails, for they are not so fast as steamers with side wheels.

Whatever may be said of the different kinds of bladed screw propellers, there does not seem to be one superior to the Woodcroft Propeller. The Sarah Sands and the City of Glasgow are fitted with this kind, and they are the only two steamships which have attempted the regular navigation of the Atlantic. The latter steam propeller has done wonders: its success has induced the contemplation of a "Line of Propellers" by a powerful company, to ply in the merchant service, between New-York and Liverpool.

The question of exclusive steam navigation is only one of economy, and the auxiliary screw propeller presents advantages in this respect, which are worthy of serious consideration by all those engaged in the shipping business.

The city of Philadelphia is the seat of constructing American Propellers, and there the "Loper Propeller," is the favorite. At the present moment, at a single establishment in Kensington, of Messrs. Reaney, Neafe & Co., machinery is now in the progress of construction for nine "Loper Propellers." This shows in what a favorable light this propeller is regarded.

BEADON'S PROPELLER.

This is rather a singular propeller in form. It is the invention of Commander Beadon, R.N., and was patented in 1846. The arms for the blades formed one of the claims. The scroll form of the arms on which to attach the blades, will be familiar to every millwright who is acquainted with Whitelaw and Stirratt's water wheel. The scroll arms have been claimed as being superior to the radial arms, and also attaching the blades directly to the shaft, owing to the extremities of screw propellers being the most effective portions of them. This is a fact, as it has been found expedient to reduce the blades of propellers (as much as is possible, consistent with strength) near to the shaft. Curved blades have also been preferred to the flat, so as to act only tangentially against the water. The rotate curve is given to the arm, increasing gradually from the centre, as in a volute.

Fig. 78.

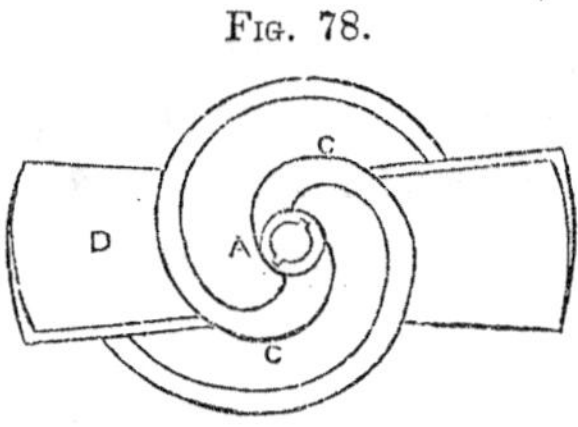

A is the shaft; C C are the curved arms; D D the propelling blade. Two curved arms may be used to support the blade.

The form of a blade essentially different from Ericson and others, has also been proposed by the same inventor, and this is represented in

FIG. 79.

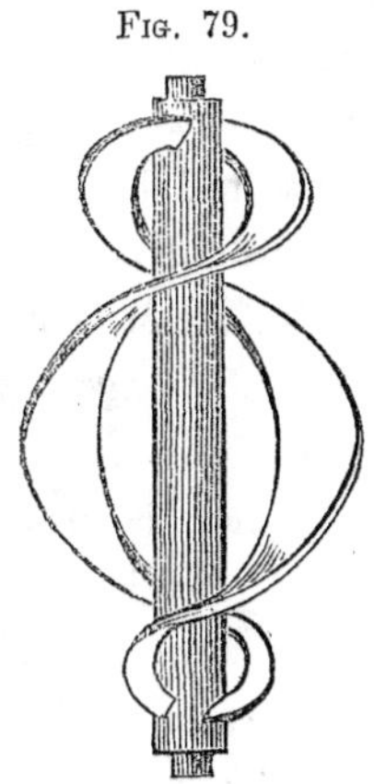

and is held to be a double propeller. The blades are secured to a long boss at each end, and the form of them, instead of being the mere segment of a screw, is that of a spheroid.

There are as many different opinions about propellers as there are about water wheels, and we have shown what a beautiful variety there is—the only way to do good.

In connection with the above English propeller, we have heard that a somewhat unique propeller has been invented there by a Mr. McIntosh, of Sheffield. It is called "McIntosh's Improved Flexible Propeller." It is made of steel, well hammered and tempered, and set on an angle on the revolving shaft. When at rest, it is a perfect plane, but when in action it forms a screw, and by the flexibility of the steel, assumes a finer or coarser pitch according to the strength of the adverse action of the water through which it moves. This circumstance imparts to the vessel and machinery an easy action, especially in a rough and heavy sea, which has never been attained by the rigid screws now in use. Propellers manufactured according to this patent are not more than half the weight of those made of cast metal, though the forgings are the largest yet attempted to be made from steel. It has been ascertained by experiment, that in point of speed there is at least twenty per cent. gained. In a heavy sea or rough weather this propeller can be easily hoisted on board by means of a simple block and tackle, thus saving the expense of the machinery now used for raising the cast metal ones; and, from being malleable and tough, does away with the risk of breakage which necessarily ensues in the moving of a cumbersome piece of cast-metal. In cost there is a saving of about fifty per cent. This is considered one of the greatest improvements yet made in marine propulsion. Four of these propellers have already been made and brought into use, and as a proof of the high estimation in which they are held, it may be stated that (the Lords of the Admiralty have ordered) her Majesty's steam-vessel Bee, the swiftest screw-vessel afloat, is to be fitted out with one of these propellers in preference to the rigid screw.

A very simple and beautiful propeller has been invented

and patented by Alexander Bond, of Philadelphia. It is a Sculling Propeller, and has only one blade. Alternately it is moved by a very ingenious mechanism from side to side of the keel at the stern, slipping forward parallel with its edge against the water alongside of the keel, and then striking backwards at an angle of about 45°.

CHAPTER VIII.

RIVER STEAMBOATS.

In America the river steamboat differs materially from the marine steamship. This difference is unknown in Britain, because the rivers there are so near the sea, that all the steamboats have been and must be built to withstand its buffetings.

The accompanying engraving is a vertical section of the American Condensing Engine, for river boats. A minute description of all the parts is not required, as our object is mainly to show its application to propulsion; nevertheless, this view of the engine will serve to convey a very correct idea of its relative parts. A is the steam cylinder; B is the piston rod passing up through a stuffing box and connected with the beam; C is the steam pipe coming from the boiler; O is the steam chest, and J is one of the rods to operate the valves; D is the injection pipe, which communicates with the water through the bottom of the boat, and it enters into the condenser, S, below the cylinder; E is the air pump which draws off the water and air in the condenser into a reservoir,

Fig. 80.

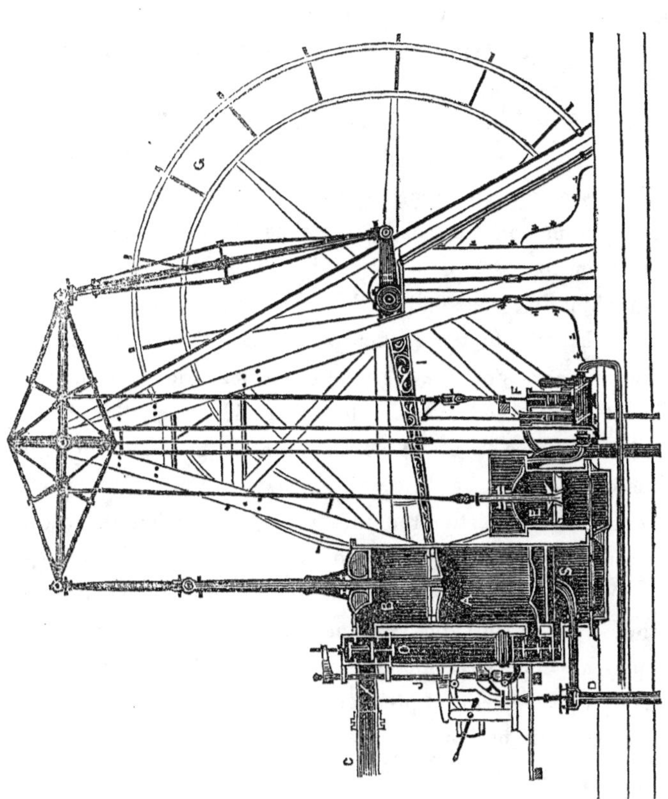

whence it passes down a pipe through the bottom of the boat. A continual stream of water rushes up the pipe, D, into the condenser, to condense the steam *suddenly*, to form a vacuum; F is a force pump, to supply the boiler with water; H is a crank secured on the main or wheel shaft, and attached by a pin to the connecting rod of the beam. On the main shaft is a rocking rod, I, which runs forward and hooks over a cross shaft in front of the steam chamber. This shaft is rocked by the rod I, which is worked by an eccentric to oscilate large curved prongs or toes in front, which act upon other prongs on the rods, J, and thus lift the valves, and allow them to close. G is the paddle-wheel. When the steam is rushing in at one end of the cylinder, it is rushing out at the exhaust into the condenser, at the other. There are four valve rods on one engine, two on one side work the exhaust valves, and two on the other side work the steam valves. These open and close alternately, giving motion to the beam, which, by the crank H, changes the reciprocating motion of the piston rod into rotary motion on the main shaft, thus propelling the paddle-wheels.

When steamboats were first built, it was supposed that they were fit only for river navigation,—this was Fulton's opinion. The great inland navigation of the United States has been the means of producing a class of steamboats which are perfectly national, and which have no rivals for speed and splendor in the world.

It is generally conceded that we are more indebted to R. L. Stevens, of New-York, for improvements in our river boats, than to any other person. It is indeed true, that we see in the above condensing engine nothing more than the principles embraced in that of Watt—excepting the manner of working the valves by "Stevens' Cut Off," which is very superior to the old tappet arrangement of Watt's engine, as is also the upright guides for the piston rod, which is superior to the parallel motion,—this also was introduced by Stevens.

The engines of the American river boats are worked on the principle of the Cornwall Engines—the stroke of the piston being long, and the steam used expansively. This is an economical practical advantage. Mr. Adam, of West Point Foundry, was the gentleman, as stated by Prof. Renwick, who introduced this system.

The form of the American steamboat is beautiful and clean for speed: they have fine clean runs, and bows like razors. They divide the water instead of pushing it up before them, and they are so long, that the divided element gradually unites towards the stern, pushing forward the vessel, instead of forming a partial vacuum behind, as in the old-fashioned short blunt boats. They are long and narrow, some being in length twelve times more than in breadth of beam.

There is one peculiarity about the American river steamboats, viz., their huge wheel-houses. The paddle-wheels of the New World, which runs in the North River, are 46 feet in diameter. The Alida is another fast boat, has wheels 31½ feet diameter, and the Thomas Powell, a smaller boat by a great deal than either of the other two, has 40-feet wheels. There does not appear to be any adopted rule for the size of the wheels according to the size of the vessel.

The Lake and River navigation of America are unequalled in any other land under the sun. It may be said, that the United States of America enjoy both a home and foreign commerce within themselves. The number of steamboats navigating all their waters, cannot be less than 2000 at the present moment. They are all propelled as represented in figure 81. The engines employed are the high and low pressure kind. All of them would employ the condensing engine if it were not for the little draught which is necessary for the navigation of some of the shallow rivers. The accidents by the high pressure boats, are as two to one in comparison with the low pressure. This should cause their abandonment as a matter of humanity.

The American river boats often run at a speed of over 20 miles an hour, and some of them can make 30 miles.

Scott Russell says respecting American River Steamboats, "they stand in every respect—in science, in speed, in beauty, in magnitude—unparalleled by the river steamers of Britain, or those of any other country."

For the past fifteen years we have noticed a gradual enlargement of the paddle-wheels on the finest river steamboats, and there has been a gradual increase of speed.

Large wheels allow the paddles to enter the water nearer to a vertical position and to rise in the same manner, than small wheels, hence there is less concussion when they enter the water, and less lift of water on the blade when rising, and these are important advantages in propelling. Aside from all theorizing, practice has proven the truth of this conclusion.

CHAPTER IX.

OCEAN NAVIGATION—THE MARINE STEAM ENGINE.

AFTER Henry Bell had established steamboat navigation in Europe, it was still a question whether they could or could not be employed for open sea navigation. Nautical men entertained the opinion that they were unfit for any other than smooth water and sunshine voyages. There was one man, however, who thought differently. This was George Dodd, a London engineer, and a young man of great resolution. He went down to Scotland and purchased the Argyle steamboat, which used to ply between Glasgow and Greenock, 20 miles. She was 79 feet keel, 16 feet beam, had an engine of 14 horse power, and her paddle-wheels were nine feet in diameter. Messrs. Wood, of Greenock were the builders. She was purchased by a company to run on the Thames, and cost about 15,000 dollars.

The vessel was exclusively appropriated to the conveyance of passengers. The engine occupied the middle of the vessel, the boiler being placed on the starboard side, and the cylinder and fly-wheel on the larboard. The smoke was carried off by a funnel, which also did duty as a mast, and carried a large square sail. It seems, indeed, to have been the anxious wish of the constructors of the early steamboats, to disguise the ugly, smoking chimney, under the designation of a mast, and some even went so far as to raise up a topmast in the thick folds of the dense smoke.

His crew consisted of a mate, four seamen, an engineer, a stoker, and a cabin-boy. It was not without heavy misgivings on the part of many persons in Glasgow, that Dodd started for his long voyage; but, full of confidence in his vessel and crew, he boldly put to sea in May, 1815. The commencement of his voyage was far from auspicious, the weather was most unfavorable, and the sea ran extremely high in the narrow channel separating Scotland from Ireland. In consequence of the negligence or misunderstanding of the pilot, who had altered the course of the vessel during the night, they ran a great risk of being wrecked. At break of day a heavy gale was blowing, and it was discovered, that instead of being off the coast of Ireland, they were within half a league of a lee rock-bound shore, two miles to the north of Port Patrick. It blew too hard to attempt to beat off by the united power of sails and steam; Dodd, therefore, depending entirely on the power of his engine, laid the vessel's head directly to windward, and ordered the log to be kept constantly going. It was soon ascertained, to the great satisfaction of all on board, that the vessel was clearing the shore and going direct in the wind's eye at the rate of three knots and a half. When he had acquired a sufficient offing, he bore away, and gained the Irish coast. Dodd was firmly of opinion that no other power than that of steam could have saved the vessel from destruction. He now continued his voyage to Dublin, where he determined to remain for a short time, to rest his crew and to examine the machinery.

While the Thames (old Argyle) was lying in Dublin bay, a spirited Irish gentleman and his lady resolved to go along with Dodd to London. This gentleman (named Weld) wrote an account of the voyage afterwards, which is, perhaps, the most remarkable on record. The sea was very rough after she left Dublin, and some naval officers who were on board, were unanimous in declaring it to be their firm opinion that the vessel could not live long in heavy seas, and that there would be much danger in venturing far from shore.

The motion of the vessel differed essentially from that of a sailing vessel; the action of the wheels on the water at each side prevented her rolling. The most disagreeable movement was felt when the waves struck the vessel on the beam; but even then her particular construction was advantageous, for the coverings which inclosed the wheels acted as buoys, and contributed to keep the vessel afloat. On such occasions the noise produced by the sudden compression of the air within the wheel-boxes was frightful. After having sustained a concussion on one side, a second was generally felt on the other, by a sort of reaction, and a third, but much more feeble, succeeded, after which the vessel preserved a regular motion for several minutes. This somewhat alarmed the passengers; but as these concussions only extended to three or four successively, all alarm soon vanished, for they saw that the vessel soon righted, and bounded lightly over the waves. All the sailing vessels which left Dublin with it, by the same tide, were soon left behind, for the weather was stormy and bad. During the passage one of the blades of the starboard paddle-wheel became out of order; the engine was stopped, and the blade was cut away. Some hours after, a similar accident happened to the other wheel, which was remedied in the same manner. The loss of one blade in each paddle made no apparent difference in the progress of the vessel. From Dublin they sailed to Milford Haven, in England, where Dodd determined to examine the boiler, which had not been done since he left Glasgow. When it was opened, a considerable quantity of fine salt was found in it, and it became necessary to clean the boiler again during the voyage.

She left Milford Haven and went into Plymouth harbor. The harbor-master, who had never seen a steam-vessel before, was as much struck with astonishment when he boarded the Thames, as a child is in getting possession of a new plaything. He steered the vessel round several ships of war in the bay. The sailors ran in crowds to the side of their vessels, and mounting the rigging, gave vent to their observations in a most amusing manner. Dodd entered the harbor in the most splendid style; steaming in, with the assistance of the wind and tide, at the rate of from twelve to fourteen miles an hour. A court-martial was at the time sitting on board the Gladiator frigate, but the novelty of the steamboat presented an irresistible attraction; and the whole court came off, excepting the president, who was obliged, by etiquette, to retain his seat until the court was regularly adjourned.

From Portsmouth, Dodd proceeded to London, and passed every thing on the Thames, astonishing all the fast-sailing boats on the river. The Thames was regarded with no little wonder by all the Londoners. She had run 758 miles in five days and two hours, and experienced during that time some severe weather, and heavy seas. It proved, incontestably, the superiority of the steamboat over the sailing vessel.

And when we remember that this was the first steamer that attempted the seas, and that she was only fourteen horse power, it must be allowed that some courage was requisite to embark in so frail a vessel for so long a voyage.

Dodd, in his examination before a Committee of the House of Commons in 1815, states, that the Thames carried fifteen tons of coals, and that the consumption was generally one ton for every hundred miles; he, however, ran the vessel from Portsmouth to Margate, a distance of one hundred and twenty nine nautical miles, with only one ton. It appears singular, that with such satisfactory practical evidence in favor of steam navigation, steamboats were not at once employed to carry the mails between England and Ireland. The Parliamentary Committee, to their credit, recommended steam packets; and Mr. Dodd, on behalf of himself and some friends, offered to be at the expense of building two steamboats, provided he was guaranteed the conveyance of the mails, in the event of the packets fully answering his representations. To this spirited offer no further attention was given by Government than the usual formal letter of acknowledgment, and it was not until 1821 that steam vessels were regularly established as post-office packets on that station: they were intended, in the first instance, merely as auxiliaries to the sailing packets, but they soon superseded them.

Many will ask, "What became of Dodd?" Alas, he died in prison, a drunkard and a beggar. He was the projector of the Thames Tunnel, which was finished by Brunel. Although possessed of great talents and courage, he was unfortunate, took to the cup, and starved himself in a fit of partial insanity, within the walls of a London prison.

The regular establishment of ocean steam navigation commenced with the Rob Roy, a steamer of about thirty horse-power and ninety tons burden, which commenced running in 1818, between Greenock and Belfast. This vessel was established by Mr. David Napier, who was highly instrumental in improving and advancing steam navigation. The Rob Roy plied for two winters with perfect regularity and success, and was afterwards transferred to the English Channel, to serve as a packet-boat between Dover and Calais. From that period steam navigation progressed most rapidly, and to no living man is the world so much indebted for this as to Mr. D. Napier (not Robert Napier, who also has done a great deal for steam navigation, but his cousin, now of London). Before Mr. Napier built the Rob Roy, he made a voyage to Ireland in one of the sailing packets, to behold a wintry storm on that tempestuous sea. He stationed himself at the bow of the vessel until the waves broke in sheets over him, and until he was informed, that it was one of the roughest passages the Captain had ever experienced; then his eye flashed, and he exclaimed, "I think *I can manage this.*" Next year, 1818, he had his steamboat running regularly between Glasgow and Belfast. He was the first engineer who introduced those kind of engines in steamships, which still hold the highest place in every respect, as being the best for snugness, convenience, and general economy.

Fig. 82 is a marine "Side Lever Steam Engine," as applied to navigation. It is different from that of the River Boat, inasmuch as the beam is below, secured on centres, at the bottom of the cylinder. The machinery of the steamship has to be under cover, low down, and snug. Every part has to be made strong, and all fitted together with the utmost care and exactness. A is the cylinder, B is the slide-valve casing, C the condenser, D the hot well, and air vessels placed on the top of the condenser. The air pump is placed below the feed pump F, K is the piston rod of the cylinder, I is the cross-head, H is one of the cylinder side rods, which descends to the beam or side lever G, L is one of the rods of the parallel motion, V is the weigh-shaft, on

Fig. 82.

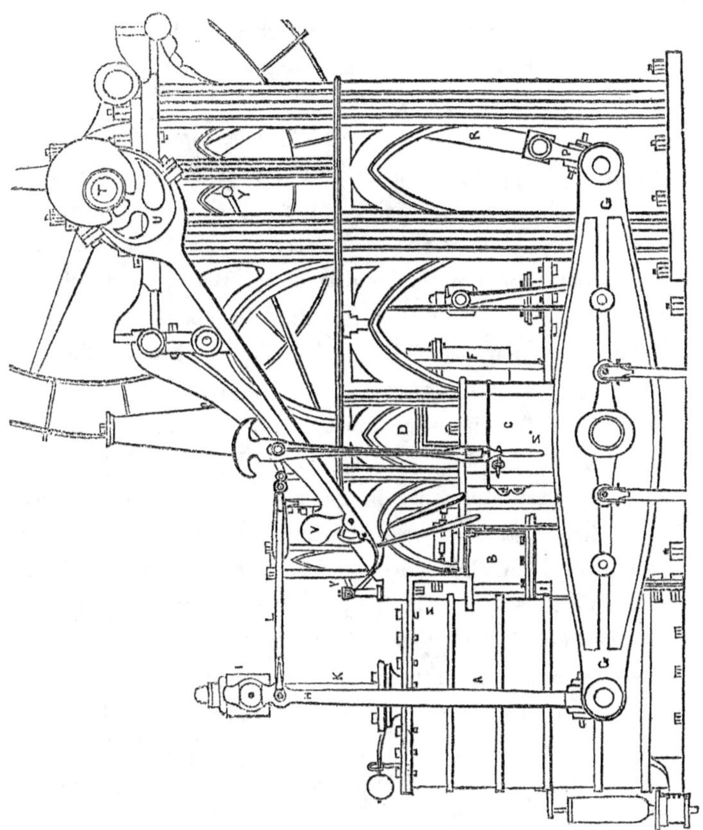

which is fixed the valve lever, the other end of which is inserted in the slide-valve link. The bilge and brine pumps are below the beam, and worked by rods attached to it. To the extremity of the beam are attached the links P, of the cross-tail, which are attached to the connecting rod R: T is the paddle-wheel shaft, U is the eccentric to work the valve by the eccentric rod: Y is the expansive valve apparatus. This figure is designed to show the difference between the mode of applying the power of the steam to propel the wheels of river and ocean vessels. The above is a side elevation of the engine of the Britannia, which so successfully navigated the Atlantic for about nine years. There is no new principle involved in the construction of the engine on the newest and best steamships. There is but very little difference in the above engine from that of the United Kingdom, built by David Napier, in 1822.

The first steamship which crossed the Atlantic from America to Europe was an American vessel named the SAVANNAH, built by Crocker & Fickitt, at Corlear's Hook, in New-York. She was built by a company of gentlemen, with a view of selling her to the Emperor of Russia. This company was organized through the agency of Capt. Moses Rogers, afterwards her commander. The Savannah was a vessel of 380 tons, ship-rigged, and was furnished with a horizontal engine. This was placed between decks—boilers in the lower hold.

The Savannah sailed from New-York, in the year 1819. She first went to Savannah. The passage occupied seven days, four of which she was under steam. There she was chartered by the corporation, as an act of courtesy, to proceed to Charleston for the purpose of affording President Monroe, who was then travelling through the States, with a pleasure excursion. For some reason, he failed to go, and the steamer returned to Savannah,—forming, while there, an object of much attraction. From Savannah, she proceeded direct to Liverpool, where she arrived after a passage of 18 days, during seven of which she was under steam.

When about entering St. George's Channel, off the city of Cork, she was descried by the commander of the British fleet, then lying at that city. Seeing a huge mass of smoke ascending from the vessel, enveloping her rigging and overshadowing the sky, he naturally inferred that a vessel was on fire in distress, and with commendable promptitude despatched two cutters to her relief. After passing near to her a few times, taking a full survey, and firing a few guns across her stern, the steamer was boarded. Finally, being perfectly satisfied that all was right, the cutters bore away.

The news of her approach having been telegraphed to Liverpool, as she drew near the city, with her sails furled and the American colors flying, the pier-heads were thronged by many thousand persons, who greeted her with the most enthusiastic cheers. Before she came to anchor, the decks were so crowded that it was with difficulty that the men could move from one part to another, in the performance of their duty. She was afterwards visited by many persons of distinction, and departed for Elsinore, on her way to St.

Petersburg.—She next touched at Copenhagen, where she remained two weeks. From Copenhagen, she went to Cronstadt and St. Petersburg. Not being able to get over the bar at the latter place, she lay opposite the city, six miles distant.

Here, as at other places, she was an object of much wonderment. She, however, was not sold, as had been expected, and sailed for home, putting into Errington, on the coast of Norway, on the passage. From the latter place, she was 22 days in reaching Savannah. On account of the high price of fuel, she carried no steam on the return passage, and the wheels were taken off. A similar course was adopted during a portion of the time occupied by the passage out from the United States. As it was nearly or quite impossible to carry sufficient fuel for the voyage, during pleasant weather the wheels were removed, and canvas substituted. On nearing Liverpool, the more effectually to "astonish the natives," the wheels were restored. At the completion of this voyage, the Savannah was divested of her steam apparatus, and used as a packet between Savannah and New-York. She subsequently went ashore on Long Island, and broke up.

Although Capt. Rogers was offered $100,000 for her, by the King of Sweden, to be paid in hemp and iron, delivered at New-York, Philadelphia, and Boston, the offer was not accepted—the cash being wanted. It is said that $50,000 or $60,000 was sunk in this transaction.

From all the descriptions given of the Savannah, her steam was only auxiliary to her sails, and her engine does not appear to have been capable of forming regular communication between the two continents, but her voyage established not only the feasibility, but the possibility of Atlantic Steam Navigation, and it is somewhat singular that no other steamship made the voyage for nineteen years after; for there is no doubt but plenty of the steamships running in the St. George's and British Channels, were perfectly able to do so.

It is now twelve years since the Atlantic was first bridged by regular steam communication between England and America.

On the morning of the 23d of April, 1838, the British steamships Sirius and Great Western entered the harbor of New-York from England. The former was the first to arrive, and may consequently be considered the first British steamer that ever entered the United States as a regular trader.

Shortly after this, the Royal Mail or Cunard Steamers, all built in Scotland and their engines constructed by Robert Napier, commenced to run between Liverpool, Halifax, and Boston. These vessels have been models of punctuality and success, but without the patronage of Government it is doubtful if they would have been successful, in point of profit. The first vessels of this line have been superseded by a larger and superior class, the engines of which are all built on the same principle as the one in figure 82, but not of the same pattern—they having wrought instead of Gothic cast-iron frames.

It is but a very few years since America constructed her

first Ocean Steamship. From the port of New-York, there are now two American Lines running to Europe. The one to Liverpool consists of the Atlantic and Pacific,—Collins' American Line—the largest steamships in the world. They have side-lever engines, and the paddle-wheels are 36 feet in diameter. The newest steamers of the Cunard Line are not so large, but they are very fine vessels. There appears to be a generous rivalry between these two lines. It is to be hoped, that it will always be tempered with prudence and energy at the same time; and, by that means, we may expect a still greater reduction in the time required to cross the Atlantic, which has already been shortened, in twelve years, twenty-two per cent. As it is self-evident, that a small steamship is incapable of performing a long sea voyage, it is as plain, that the larger and more powerful the steamship, the shorter and more successful passage will she make; and it is not too much to expect, that, in twenty years from the present date, passages will be made from America to England in seven days, for Ocean Steam Navigation has certainly not yet attained to its "manhood's might."

CONCLUDING REMARKS.

It will be perceived, that the majority of propelling devices which have been presented in this work, were invented to prevent the lift of water by the paddle-wheel, and to make the propelling blades act less obliquely on the water than in the vertical curves, which are necessarily described by the revolving paddle-wheels. But the real action of the paddle-wheel on the water does not appear to be generally understood. It does not describe a true circle by its action in the water when the vessel is moving forward, but a cycloid, hence the paddles act far more effectually—like the motion of a carriage-wheel on a road—than is generally supposed. There is some loss by water lift, but not so much as some have imagined. By experiments with the improved Morgan paddle-wheel in smooth water, eighteen per cent. have been added to the speed of one vessel on the Clyde. This shows a drawback in the common wheel from water lift, but the feathering paddles would not answer apparently for ocean navigation. With the exception of the Morgan wheel for smooth water, (the advantages of which are secured in enlarging the wheel), no other propelling device in the foregoing pages is equal to the paddle-wheel. It can be built strong and compact. It has but few bearings, and consequently its working friction is confined to the journals of a single shaft. The paddle-wheel has proved itself to be the prince of propelling devices for speed, but as an auxiliary to sails, and as being better adapted to war, and mere cargo vessels, the screw propeller is undoubtedly to be preferred.

When we look at the mighty advances made by man in application of steam power to the arts, and especially in subduing the billows of the ocean to his sway, it requires no great faith to believe, that the time is not far distant, when every ship which navigates the ocean will use steam as a prime or auxiliary propelling power.

www.ingramcontent.com/pod-product-compliance
Lightning Source LLC
LaVergne TN
LVHW021413110826
845150LV00007B/1904

* 9 7 8 1 4 2 5 5 1 0 5 5 8 *